D1546336

# More Praise for
## *Working with Problem Faculty*

"There's a wealth of practical advice in this book for administrators at all levels. I'm going to keep a copy of *Working with Problem Faculty* close at hand because Kent Crookston provides such excellent insight into one of the most difficult challenges we all face today."

—Jeffrey L. Buller, dean of the Harriet L. Wilkes
Honors College at Florida Atlantic University,
and author, *The Essential Department Chair,*
*2nd edition* and *Best Practices in*
*Faculty Evaluation*

"Dr. Crookston is a favorite among presenters at the Academic Chairpersons Conference. His research and thought-provoking case studies focus on positive faculty relationships and provide chairs with six concrete steps that can be applied immediately."

—Kathryn Harth, program coordinator, Conferences
and Noncredit Programs, Division of Continuing
Education, Kansas State University

# WORKING WITH PROBLEM FACULTY

A Six-Step Guide for
Department Chairs

R. KENT CROOKSTON

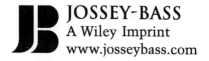

JOSSEY-BASS
A Wiley Imprint
www.josseybass.com

Published by Jossey-Bass
A Wiley Imprint
One Montgomery Street, Suite 1200, San Francisco, CA 94104-4594—www.josseybass.com

Jossey-Bass books and products are available through most bookstores. To contact Jossey-Bass directly call our Customer Care Department within the U.S. at 800-956-7739, outside the U.S. at 317-572-3986, or fax 317-572-4002.

Wiley publishes in a variety of print and electronic formats and by print-on-demand. Some material included with standard print versions of this book may not be included in e-books or in print-on-demand. If this book refers to media such as a CD or DVD that is not included in the version you purchased, you may download this material at http://booksupport.wiley.com. For more information about Wiley products, visit www.wiley.com.

*Library of Congress Cataloging-in-Publication Data*

Crookston, Robert Kent, date.
    Working with problem faculty : a six-step guide for department chairs / R. Kent Crookston.
      p.  cm.
    Includes index.
    ISBN 978-1-118-24238-4 (hardback); ISBN 978-1-118-28501-5 (ebk);
    ISBN 978-1-118-28312-7 (ebk); ISBN 978-1-118-28351-6 (ebk)
      1. College personnel management.   2. College department heads—Professional relationships.   3. Problem employees.  I. Title.
    LB2331.66.W67   2012
    378.1'1—dc23

                                               2012016812

Printed in the United States of America
FIRST EDITION
*HB Printing* 10 9 8 7 6 5 4 3 2 1

# Jossey-Bass Resources for Department Chairs

## Books

Jeffrey L. Buller, *Academic Leadership Day by Day: Small Steps That Lead to Great Success*

Jeffrey L. Buller, *The Essential Department Chair: A Comprehensive Desk Reference, Second Edition*

Jeffrey L. Buller, *Best Practices in Faculty Evaluation: A Practical Guide for Academic Leaders*

Don Chu, *The Department Chair Primer: What Chairs Need to Know and Do to Make a Difference, Second Edition*

Robert E. Cipriano, *Facilitating a Collegial Department in Higher Education: Strategies for Success*

R. Kent Crookston, *Working with Problem Faculty: A Six-Step Guide for Department Chairs*

Christian K. Hansen, *Time Management for Department Chairs*

Mary Lou Higgerson, *Communication Skills for Department Chairs*

Mary Lou Higgerson and Teddi A. Joyce, *Effective Leadership Communication: A Guide for Department Chairs and Deans for Managing Difficult Situations and People*

Deryl Leaming, *Academic Leadership: A Practical Guide to Chairing the Department, Second Edition*

Deryl Leaming, *Managing People: A Guide for Department Chairs and Deans*

N. Douglas Lees, *Chairing Academic Departments: Traditional and Emerging Expectations*

Darla J. Twale and Barbara M. De Luca, *Faculty Incivility: The Rise of the Academic Bully Culture and What to Do About It*

Jon Wergin, *Departments That Work: Building and Sustaining Cultures of Excellence in Academic Programs*

Daniel W. Wheeler et al., *The Department Chair's Handbook, Second Edition*

Daniel W. Wheeler, *Servant Leadership for Higher Education: Principles and Practices*

## Journals

*The Department Chair*

*The Life Cycle of a Department Chair: New Directions for Higher Education, No. 126,* Walter H. Gmelch (Editor), John H. Schuh (Editor)

## Online Resources

Visit www.departmentchairs.org for information on online seminars, articles, book excerpts, and other resources tailored especially for department chairs.

# Contents

---

Problem Faculty: The Number One Concern
of America's Academic Chairs    1

## Part One    The Six Steps

## Part Two    Tough Questions

# Contents

# WORKING WITH
# PROBLEM FACULTY

# Problem Faculty: The Number One Concern of America's Academic Chairs

In a recent survey, almost three thousand American academic chairs identified tasks for which they wanted help or information.[1] Out of twenty tasks, "dealing with problem faculty" was the strong first choice. The other top selections were, in descending order, guiding department change, evaluating faculty and staff, nourishing department climate, and managing conflicts. Notice that each of the top five selections involves people-to-people interactions that are often accompanied by tension or trauma and in which the behavior of one or more individuals may be problematic for someone else.

When chairs talk about problem faculty, what are their specific concerns? What are the most challenging issues? What can a chair do to "fix" things? Drawing on the wisdom of numerous chairs, the academic-leadership literature, and my own experience as a department head and dean, I have developed a perspective and collected a few stories about the nature and extent of problem faculty issues in American higher education and have identified six steps that I recommend for academic chairs when dealing with colleagues who are problematic for them.

Note that I do not offer six *easy* steps for dealing with the top concern of America's academic chairs. Dealing with problem faculty was selected most often by three thousand chairs for a reason: succeeding with a challenging colleague can be difficult and in some cases impossible. It takes patience and lots of work, and some of that work lies beyond the jurisdiction of the chair. The situation is made all the more frustrating by the fact that the overall academic culture usually bears much more responsibility for one person's deviant conduct than the chair does. This includes the previous chairs and deans, the HR office, the director of faculty relations, and the bulk of the colleagues within the department. Comments from chairs in the national survey reinforce several specific realities that make it daunting for a chair to deal with problem colleagues:

- **Chairs often see themselves as temporary custodians and servants, not as controllers.** "I have always tried to keep in mind," one chair noted, "that my primary role is not to police my colleagues but to serve and that my position as chair is not a lifetime appointment but a momentary one in my career."

- **Campus culture and politics often provide little support for a chair who takes corrective action.** "Faculty want their leaders to do the things they can't or won't do themselves but offer little support when the heavy stuff comes down (lawsuits, inquires, etc.). I've come to view faculty governance and faculty integrity when it comes to these issues as hopeless."

- **The chair who stands up to a challenging colleague can actually be vilified.** "Personnel decisions and dealing with problem faculty are the most nettlesome issues, and I can't say that I ever dealt with them very well. The faculty usually want something done, but when you do something, they are often nowhere to be seen and blame the whole thing on you."

Pood describes the predicament well: "What started out as an attempt on the part of the department chair to discuss and correct a behavior on the part of one of his or her faculty members has suddenly become a referendum on the skills and qualifications of the chair!"[2]

The purpose of this book is not to document the nature and extent of the challenge and frustration, however, but rather to share what survey participants and authorities on chairing have suggested for managing it.

## ∿ "Problem Faculty" Defined ∿

There are numerous descriptions of problem faculty in the chair literature. Higgerson and Joyce identify "pot stirrers/troublemakers" (who raise issues without suggesting solutions), "prima donna/drama queens" (who command the spotlight and are never wrong), "confrontation junkies" (who create and fuel conflicts), and "passive and indifferent souls" (who resist change and taking any action).[3] Bissell cites "complainers," "procrastinators," "guerrilla fighters" (they insult others in public), "experts" (they refuse to be wrong), and "icicles" (they freeze up at the sight of conflict).[4] In addition to these more egregious characters, chairs must often deal with more passive yet still difficult faculty, such as underperformers who are just doing the bare minimum, faculty who make end runs around the chair, senior faculty who have gone into retirement mode while they are still on the full-time payroll, faculty who have great promise but do not rise to their potential, faculty who are bad teachers, and faculty who make little effort to get along with their colleagues.

Altman's observation is appropriate:

> Most academics (and academic administrators) can point to one or more faculty members on their campus whose job performance and/or relationships with others have changed for the worse. In this sense, while a comprehensive definition of troubled faculty may be hard to pin down, most of us assume we know one when we see one.[5]

However we define them, difficult members of the faculty are typically in the minority yet often demand a disproportionate amount of a chair's time. Fischer notes that negative interactions have five times the impact of positive ones, the influence of a "few destructive individuals dwarfs their number, and the damage they do keeps accruing."[6]

If the catalogue of troublesome characters and their impact on departments seems overwhelming, don't despair. The same experts who drew up these character lists have suggested ways to succeed with (or adjust to) such individuals, to encourage them into compliance, and to develop their strengths and minimize their deficiencies. Their solutions and my own form the core of this book.

## ∿ An Important Question Before We Start ∿

How should a chair view the challenge of problem faculty? One view might be that a difficult person is an isolated deviant and that things can be made right when corrective measures have reformed the person or when the person has been removed.

A different outlook is that the existence of a problem faculty member is a sign that the entire department needs to mend itself and adopt new expectations and practices. I believe that if a department is experiencing behavior on the part of one or more faculty members that is problematic to others, there's probably some collective adaptive work to be done by most if not all of the people in that department.

Shortly after becoming a dean, I attended a workshop at Harvard on dealing with problem colleagues. We considered an incident that led to the firing of a staff member in the office of a large college. The dean had gathered the staff and asked them to consider where *they* had messed up. He didn't spend any time discussing how the person just fired had messed up, but rather began asking such questions as "Who hired her?" "Who trained her?" "To whom did she report?" and "With whom did she interact?" He then said, "All of us have failed," and pointed out that it would be a mistake to hire a replacement until they discovered how they could get things right. "We haven't made any internal improvement by letting her go," the dean said. "If we rehire without changing the way we do things, we may just end up firing the next one."

In the afternoon session of that workshop, we spent two hours considering the types of things a department might do to deal with a person who's become a problem. I grew frustrated with what seemed indirect if not evasive tactics and asked, "When do you just say enough is enough and take the person out?"

"Never" was the facilitator's response. "Don't even go there." He then explained that if you rely on dismissal as a remedy, you'll solve nothing. By simply removing the problem without attending to and fixing the system that allowed and nurtured it, you will only have created a vacancy for the next problem-in-waiting.

I believe that both the dean and the workshop facilitator were wise in their conclusion that if any department hopes to remediate problem behavior occurring within it, the entire unit, led by the chair, must collectively engage in corrective conduct. Simply throwing a deviant colleague off the bus is not a sustainable solution.

## Notes

1. R. K. Crookston. (2010). Results from a national survey: The help chairs want most. *The Department Chair*, *21*(1), 13–15.

2. E. A. Pood. (2003). Stripping away negative defenses. In D. R. Leaming (Ed.), *Managing people: A guide for department chairs and deans* (p. 99). Bolton, MA: Anker.

3. M. L. Higgerson & T. A. Joyce. (2007). *Effective leadership communication: A guide for department chairs and deans for managing difficult situations and people.* Bolton, MA: Anker.

4. B. Bissell. (2003). Handling conflict with difficult faculty. In D. R. Leaming (Ed.), *Managing people: A guide for department chairs and deans* (chap. 8). Bolton, MA: Anker.

5. H. B. Altman. (2003). Dealing with troubled faculty. In D. R. Leaming (Ed.), *Managing people: A guide for department chairs and deans* (p. 141). Bolton, MA: Anker.

6. M. Fischer. (2009). Defending collegiality. *Change*, *41*(3), 25.

# PART ONE

# The Six Steps

A major goal of the chair is to create a positive and productive department where creativity is encouraged and interactivity thrives. This often happens best when the challenges and friction that result from diversity in specialties, training, background, and personality are exploited and applied to productive ends. I have identified six steps that can help bring about better relationships and productivity in an academic unit, even with difficult people.

• **Step 1: Clarify values and expectations.** When the members of a department community have taken the time to identify what guides and inspires them, as well as the productivity and etiquette they expect of one another, it is relatively easy for a chair to confront an individual's performance that is deviant.

• **Step 2: Follow policy.** Every campus has policy and procedures for conducting research; hiring and firing; dealing with disability, discrimination, sexual harassment; and other matters. Knowing and following these policies is essential when dealing with problem situations and people.

• **Step 3: Build trust with colleagues.** The chair who has developed a trusting relationship with the right people has little to fear when proceeding to resolve a problem with any individual. And the problem person is in fact one of the "right" people.

• **Step 4: Evaluate yourself and your perceptions.** Seriously considering whether you are partly to blame for the conduct of a colleague who exasperates you and how you might modify your thinking to deal effectively with that person can be very difficult. But examining whether you may be part of the problem is a big first step toward doing something about resolving it.

• **Step 5: Listen.** Listening effectively was the top recommendation for chairing offered by participants in the national survey. Effective listening is not easy, especially when we believe the other person is a jerk, but it can be one of the most powerful ways to find solutions to problem behavior.

• **Step 6: Take effective action.** Taking effective action could be a component of each of the previous steps, but it is so important that it warrants its own chapter. Effective action consists of being prepared and confronting challenging people with consideration and composure.

Each of these steps is developed separately in the six chapters in Part One. Each chapter begins with and is developed around an authentic decision case or dilemma common to academic chairing that illustrates the guiding principles associated with the step. A summary of step-specific recommendations is provided at the end of each chapter.

# CHAPTER ONE

# Step 1: Clarify Values and Expectations

## Anna

*Anna had just been appointed chair. Walter was a senior member of the faculty with an international reputation for scholarship. He had just acted badly in a department meeting, using ridicule and sarcasm to belittle a colleague who was proposing a modification of the curriculum. No one stood up to him. After the meeting, Anna and two of her close colleagues were gathered in Anna's office. They were angry. Their anger was less with Walter than with themselves. Among their comments were "We let him get away with it again," "He's carried on like this for too many years," and "Anna, you're the chair now; you've got to do something."*

What would you think if you were Anna? Wouldn't you feel defensive and wonder, "Why me?" Wouldn't you be frustrated that previous chairs had not stood up to Walter? If Anna did decide to act, what should she do? Should she go to Walter's office and confront him? Maybe she should have confronted him in front of everybody. But how could she have done that and not just made matters worse? Actually, she probably already did make matters worse in that she essentially condoned his behavior by saying nothing. Now all of the rest of the faculty, including her two close colleagues, had been let down.

Because Anna's case is real (she was chair of an English Department), we have the benefit of knowing what she did. After a little more venting, the three colleagues realized that what they needed was a departmental behavioral code. Using the whiteboard for brainstorming, they wrote "cordiality," "no threats or insults," "be respectful," "be supportive," and "no swearing." Encouraged, they brainstormed some more individually and then regrouped, only to find that they were hesitant about bringing their work into the open. A solution came as they decided to expand their efforts to include expectations for all aspects of their work, not just civility, and to involve others, including staff and students. They started with other members of the faculty whom they expected would lend a willing hand. When they had a solid draft, Anna showed it to her dean and the faculty relations director to ensure that the code was in harmony with the university's mission and policies; the dean even asked if he could share it with other departments when it was finished. (The faculty on Anna's campus was not unionized, but if it had been, it would have been essential for her to check out union agreements and to involve a union representative in the development of the departmental code.)

## ∿ An Expectations Document ∿

"Early in my tenure, I wrote a department expectations document that was unanimously adopted by the faculty. The adoption was successful because I circulated drafts and revisions electronically among the faculty for weeks before there was any discussion in an open meeting. The document has been very valuable to our faculty and to me as I evaluate performance. I believe that it has also given starting faculty very clear guidelines for their first years in the department."

—*Survey comment*

Nine months after that first meeting in Anna's office, a "measures of excellence" document was accepted by near-unanimous vote of the department; Walter was one of only two who abstained. The following represents the major points of the document. Behavior was rated on a five-point scale, ranging from superior (5) to unacceptable (1). Level 4 and 5 performance included and built on level 3 (successful) performance.

### *Teaching*

5. **Superior** teaching, as evidenced by continual reconsideration of course learning outcomes, with valid and transparent measures consistent with program and department goals. Student ratings significantly above department averages. Highly active in mentoring students outside the class (undergraduate theses, special projects, etc.).

4. **Strong** teaching, as evidenced by creative and rigorous course design and delivery, attention to course learning outcomes and measures, attention to students outside of

class, and above-average student ratings, including narrative comments.

3. **Successful** teaching, as evidenced by efforts to revise and improve with well-considered goals, solid lesson plans, helpful and prompt feedback, and sincere concern for student learning. Student ratings near the department average. Course learning goals consistent with and supportive of program learning outcomes.

2. **Substandard** teaching, as evidenced by some combination of subpar student ratings, significant student complaints, frequent absences from class or late arrival to class, failure to provide students with prompt feedback, superficial attention to course and program learning outcomes, and/or resistance to department work on assessment.

1. **Unacceptable** teaching, as evidenced by very low teaching scores (greater than 1.5 points below department average on seven-point scale), consistent student complaints, failure to provide students with helpful and timely feedback, course content that fails to meet disciplinary standards, and/or refusal to accept proportionate share of teaching load.

## *Scholarship*

5. **Superior** scholarship by consistently publishing major monographs, collections, editions, groundbreaking articles or creative works, and the like, in prestigious publications or venues.

4. **Strong** scholarship by producing articles or creative works and presentations at high-profile conferences, with a high level of involvement in the profession (including receiving fellowships or awards, editorial service, book reviews, etc.).

3. **Successful** scholarship by averaging one peer-reviewed article or equivalent per year, with verifiable progress toward a major scholarly project (book, edition, translation). Timely and thoughtful annual reports with well-considered goals.

2. **Substandard** scholarship consisting of a trend of not publishing and with no tangible evidence of work in progress. Submits annual report, though with little thought or commitment to improvement.

1. **Unacceptable** scholarship, with no verifiable work in progress, no recent submissions, and no publications over a multiyear period. Does not willingly develop plans for improvement and shows no enthusiasm for increasing teaching or service contributions to compensate for lack of scholarly work.

## Service

5. **Superior,** diligent service to department, college, university, or profession by attending meetings and contributing constructively; includes holding leadership posts. Contributes actively and positively to the morale of the department and campus.

4. **Strong,** faithful service on major assignments or significant department, college, or university committees. Volunteers for assignments. May include national work such as editorial boards, scholarly reviewer, and assignments in national organizations.

3. **Successful** service with consistent attendance and input at most department, college, and university meetings. Available and accessible. Has well-considered goals for continuing growth as a university citizen. Uses university resources appropriately.

2. **Substandard** service including frequent absence from meetings, consistently coming late, and/or inconsistent or unreliable performance on committees. Little evidence of commitment to improvement. Questionable loyalty to unit mission evidenced by nonsupportive behavior or public comments.

1. **Unacceptable** service by failure to participate in meetings and refusal to serve on committees and to fulfill assignments. Frequently away from office and disengaged from formal and informal life of the department. Does not willingly develop plans for improvement and/or shows little or no progress on meeting expectations.

### *Collegiality*

5. **Superior** collegiality as evidenced by contributing actively and positively to the morale of the department and campus. Promotes courtesy and harmony and politely takes a stand against incivility when it occurs. Openly recognizes and promotes contributions of others in achieving department and university goals. Works for the good of the whole rather than for personal gain or credit. Is supportive of others' careers, lives, and families.

4. **Strong** collegiality based on positive interaction with others and having and assuming positive intent with all comments. Supports candid dialogue and disagrees agreeably. Open to new ideas, teachable. Optimistic, and complimentary in conversations and correspondence. Listens attentively.

3. **Successful** collegiality as evidenced by using courtesy and respect when interacting with students, staff, campus offices, administration, visitors, and professional colleagues. Supports unit mission, goals, and behavioral

norms. Keeps sensitive or private information confidential. Has a sense of humor and uses it respectfully.

2. **Substandard** collegiality as shown by minimizing mission, values, behavioral norms, or policy. Arrogant and condescending; treats colleagues, staff, and students as inferiors; ignores or excludes them. Interrupts, tells side jokes, or holds ancillary discussions in meetings. Participates in fabrications and gossip. Uses dirty looks, sarcasm, teasing.

1. **Unacceptable** collegiality as demonstrated by ignoring or violating behavioral norms or policy. Insubordinate, prejudiced, known for inflammatory statements or e-mails. Humiliates, threatens, attacks, degrades, or insults others. Fails to respect personal space; makes uninvited physical contact; uses vulgarity.

## ∿ "A Covenant That Guides Our Core Beliefs" ∿

As chair of the Department of Educational Leadership and Cultural Foundations at the University of North Carolina, Greensboro, Carol Mullen writes, "Alongside my faculty I have produced a covenant that guides our core beliefs and embeds our group's conscience, cultural values, and professional aspirations."[1] Carol clarified that the covenant was not a policy document that came down from administration with "punitive controls." Rather it was developed in-house and consisted of "an enduring promise" to one another to live by the expressed tenets. Carol and her colleagues involved everyone at all levels in the department. They obtained feedback from their dean, provost, and university attorney to ensure consistency with university policy. They viewed their covenant as a "lighthouse" which promoted the following, among other ideals:

"Individuals' continuous growth through improved experimentation with one's pedagogy and demonstrated articulation of that growth."

Prioritizing the quality of one's publications and other contributions over their quantity. "We share Albert Einstein's view that 'not everything that can be counted counts and not everything that counts can be counted.'"

Collegiality "as necessary in a community of intellectual peers for the betterment and collective governance of the department."

Like Anna's department, Carol and her colleagues agreed on specific performances and behaviors to which they were committed. It is easy to understand why Carol said that their covenant helped them find their way in the academic culture and was particularly useful when deviant behavior arose. I know from talking with Carol that no member of her faculty would claim to be ignorant of their covenant and its contents.

> "We renew our commitment to our department values annually, with faculty explaining what the values mean to them and helping our newer faculty become part of our community."
>
> —*Survey comment*

## ∿ "A Few Rules and Expectations" ∿

For twelve years Winn Egan was chair of the Department of Teacher Education at Brigham Young University. He reported that as a new chair, he soon found that the hardest part was dealing with obnoxious people, especially in meetings.[2] After he had been on the job for four years, he decided that the department needed a few rules and expectations. "Some thought it was immature to have to do that, but it got us thinking about how we wanted to be when we're together," he said. Their rules included the following:

### Participation
- Attend meetings.
- Arrive on time.
- Come prepared; follow through with all assignments.
- Be actively involved.

### Communication
- Listen; take time for full explanations.
- Work toward equity in hearing all voices.
- Be open to new ideas.
- Assume positive intent with all comments.
- Learn how to disagree agreeably.
- Don't hold back; say what needs to be said.
- Avoid side discussions.
- Realize that being heard does not always mean acceptance of the ideas.
- Seek to understand differences through dialogue and discussion.

### Social Interactions
- Be respectful and courteous.
- Avoid sarcasm.
- Learn the names of all faculty members.

- When you have difficulty with someone, talk to that person.
- Interact with new people and make them feel welcome.

"We still have conflicts," Winn says, "but now that we have our statement of understanding, they're almost all healthy ones. It's been like going from night to day. Problem behaviors have pretty much narrowed down to those that require very special one-on-one attention such as emotional instability, troubles at home, and that sort of thing."

## ～ Starting with a Vision or Mission ～

Departments don't always start where Anna's did; they develop a vision or mission statement or something like it—a clarification of their contract with society, their duties, and their core purpose. Once discovered and refined through self-examination with no one left out, this document serves as a guiding star that can unify and inspire the department.

Jody Bortone was chair of the Department of Occupational Therapy and Health Sciences at Sacred Heart University in Fairfield, Connecticut. Jody and her faculty retreated to a member's house one summer and began putting up sticky notes with words that came to mind as they discussed what was important to them and what they aspired to be. As they were arranging the words, the acronym PRIDE (for *principled, responsive, innovative, dynamic*, and *excellent*) emerged.[3] What follows is a condensed version of the vision and mission statement Jody's department developed (only one bulleted point per category is shown here; the complete statement appears in Appendix A).

## Sacred Heart University Graduate Program in Occupational Therapy

### PROGRAM'S VISION

*We are:*

PRINCIPLED
- We prioritize service to the local community, especially the uninsured, poor, children, and women.

RESPONSIVE
- The program strives to be readily available and personally attend to the needs of our students, staff, and faculty and operate in a student-centered manner.

INNOVATIVE
- The program is among the first in the University to implement cutting-edge technologies for learning and daily operation.

DYNAMIC
- The program faculty are collaborative and team-oriented and strive for diversity and dynamism in pedagogy, clinical expertise, and educational approach.

EXCELLENT
- The faculty provide service to the community, engage in continual curricular improvements and innovative design, and are committed to quality teaching, scholarship, and leadership in the profession.

*(Continued)*

## Sacred Heart University Graduate Program in Occupational Therapy (*Continued*)

### PROGRAM'S MISSION

We are committed to giving personal attention to each student in order to foster in them:

- Active engagement in promoting a just society through professional practice, leadership, and scholarship

We believe that:

- A compassionate heart is essential in all interactions with clients and communities of need

We promote a learning environment that:

- Forms collaborative partnerships between faculty, students, and clinical practitioners

Our approach to learning is to:

- Foster clinical reasoning and evidenced-based practice through self-directed, problem-based learning

Notice that Jody's faculty did not assemble a detailed definition of their territory as different from another department on campus. They did not compose a patronizing proclamation designed to impress. Instead they pinpointed the specific work and behavior that would make them proud of what they did and how they did it.

If people have a clear understanding of their unit's mission and values, they will be slower to pursue their own personal agendas. Wise is the chair who regularly reinforces the agreed priorities of the department and institution and also helps the faculty document that their work is compliant and supportive. Then with the department's statement of behavioral expectations in hand, it is relatively easy for a chair to deal with individual action or performance that is off target. If the unit's objectives and expected behaviors are unclear or unknown, the chair will likely be hesitant to confront what he feels is aberrant behavior because it will come across as "my opinion versus yours."

> "Starting every meeting with an examination of our mission and a reminder of who we are has helped keep us all moving in the same direction."
>
> —*Survey comment*

Some people think that good mission statements should be short enough for everyone to memorize. Years ago I saw a small sign framed on the wall of a Pizza Hut. It said, "The mission of Pizza Hut is to be the first place people think of when they want a pizza." I thought it was effective. One of my colleagues is a Catholic nun; her personal mission is "to improve the welfare of my soul and the souls of others." Many departments use "students first" as their mantra. Then whenever they find themselves bogged in indecision, they can pause and ask, which budgetary allocation, which curriculum adjustment, or which candidate will best serve the needs and interests of our students?

## ∿ Fun ∿

Frequently referring to and using mission statements and values can be fun. Jim Kouzes and Barry Posner recommend using celebrations to reinforce dedication to mission and to reinforce acceptable behaviors. They write:

All over the world, in every country, in every culture, people stop working on certain days during the year and take the time to celebrate. . . . Celebrations are among the most significant ways we have to proclaim our respect and gratitude, to renew our sense of community, and to remind ourselves of the values and history that bind us together.[4]

If your department has a document that spells out its mission and clarifies the behavior that people expect and value as they carry it out, you have an excellent resource to draw on as you interact with a member of the faculty who appears to be off track or out of compliance. If you don't have such a document, consider doing what chairs like Anna, Jody Bortone, Carol Mullen, and Winn Egan have done and put something together. When you're finished, refer to your document often, include it in your celebrations, and most important of all, honor it.

*Refer to your document often, include it in your celebrations, and most important of all, honor it.*

## ∿ A Word of Caution ∿

Sometimes mission statements, vision statements, goal statements, and the like can be a sham—a false store front that serves no purpose than to decorate your office or home page and waste your time. It may even become an item of ridicule as members of your unit realize it is not honored.

The key to a good mission statement is its integrity and the process by which it is created. You will not *compose* a good mission statement; you will *discover* it. It will not describe or define you; it will guide and inspire you. It will arise out of reflection on what your group identifies as most important to you at your deepest level—what motivates you to come to work early or stay late, for the good of the whole, even when there is no deadline.

## ∿ A Great Department Climate ∿

One of the principal fruits of clarifying values and expectations, *and then upholding them*, is a favorable department climate. Irene Hecht and her colleagues write the following:

> On most campuses there are in fact dozens of microenvironments with sharply divergent cultures: good-spirited, productive departments coexist alongside dysfunctional ones. As a faculty member once explained to me, "When we go to work in the morning, we go to our department." And more often than not, the morale—the tone of life in a department—is a mirror of its chair.[5]

Most chairs will likely be reluctant to accept the onus suggested in that paragraph. But if you are determined to sustain the enjoyable climate that now exists in your department, or if you feel inspired to use your term to make a transitional start from dysfunctional to great, consider that among all the suggestions in the chair literature (organize a lot of socials, walk the halls and interact with people, send personal notes, bring chocolates, attend seminars, catch people doing good things, pay compliments, and so on)—all of which are excellent practices—nothing is more foundational to a great climate than the knowledge and assurance that people who come to work in your department understand what is valued, as well as what sort of performance and behavior are expected of them, and that these expectations are upheld.

## Summary for Step 1: Clarify Values and Expectations

- Identify (through group process) your unit's mission and values.

- Clarify (through group process) behavioral norms and expectations.

- Constantly revisit, celebrate, and uphold what you identify.

- Use mission and values as a standard against which you evaluate performance and behavior; the deviant will stand out.

### Notes

1. C. A. Mullen. (2010). Promoting departmental community and civility through covenant development. *Department Chair, 20*(4), 13–16.

2. W. Egan. Personal communication, October 20, 2009.

3. J. Bortone. Personal communication, October 21, 2009.

4. J. M. Kouzes & B. Z. Posner. (2003). *The Jossey-Bass academic administrator's guide to exemplary leadership* (p. 89). San Francisco: Jossey-Bass.

5. I.W.D. Hecht, M. L. Higgerson, W. H. Gmelch, & A. Tucker. (1999). *The department chair as academic leader* (p. vii). Phoenix, AZ: Oryx Press.

# CHAPTER TWO

# Step 2: Follow Policy

## Tony

*Tony had hired Blaine from a university satellite research center that been closed. Blaine had never taught but had a Ph.D. and a reputation for getting grants and publishing. Tony had never handled a within-the-institution transfer, and his offer letter was sort of a friendly shot from the hip to a professional colleague who had been around for years and who was out of a job. The letter omitted the standard boilerplate language but did explain that Blaine would start from scratch and go through the regular tenure process, including third-year and sixth-year reviews.*

*For two years Blaine's performance was stellar; he received the department's outstanding teaching award and landed a sizable new external grant. Tony intercepted reports of his being boorish at times, offending female students with jokes and in-class comments. He considered bringing it up during annual reviews but decided to let it go unless there were recurrences. As they were assembling materials for*

*Blaine's third-year review, reports of peculiar social interactions and comments surfaced. Tony invited Blaine to his office; Blaine bristled and inflated himself noticeably as he challenged the reports as nonsense and said he had "little tolerance for incompetent administrators who perpetrated rumors and gossip." Tony was upset by the interaction and by the way Blaine could intimidate.*

*Blaine received unanimous support from the faculty for his third-year review, and Tony wrote a supportive letter. Over the next year Tony received several specific written complaints about Blaine from women students; he turned them over to the equal opportunity office. The EEO conducted a thorough investigation and concluded that in at least three instances, Blaine's conduct constituted sexual harassment. To Tony's surprise, both the EEO and the legal office had other complaints in their files from Blaine's days in the research center. After several consultations that included the dean and senior administrators, it was decided that Blaine's contract would not be renewed at the end of his fifth year. Blaine sued for wrongful dismissal, maintaining, among other things, that Tony's letter promised him a sixth-year review.*

Tony's case typifies a well-meaning chair who became lax in following policy; here's a brief summary of what we can learn from his experience.

Chairs are among the individuals who must be mindful of the concept of "apparent authority." Tony had neither the intention nor the power to promise Blaine a sixth-year review. But since he was Blaine's "boss," Blaine relied on what Tony wrote as binding, and courts usually view it the same way.

There may be hundreds of "loose" letters written at universities across the country that never result in trouble because the people to whom they are written do not become problematic. Don't let the exception be yours. Whenever you wing it, what you write can, and in a contest usually will, be held against you.

Issues governed by policy are almost always complicated and difficult; Tony tried to make things easy and friendly. There are untold ways that a person can mess up or overlook a detail when in policy territory. If all jots and tittles are followed scrupulously, and if the critical players (dean, HR, associate provost) are consulted, there's little wiggle room left for contesting what was done. If the people in HR or the legal office had reviewed Tony's letter, they would have spotted his omissions in a heartbeat.

The components of policy not only provide protection but also provide a wedge against the institution when they are not followed. When confronted with "Why did you not follow policy?" a defendant chair faces the presumption that he or she was either sloppy or discriminatory.

In university dismissal cases that are challenged, whether for misconduct or failure to earn tenure, the basis of that challenge is almost always either that process was not followed or that policy was applied in a discriminatory manner; otherwise the strength of the challenge consists of no

> *When confronted with "Why did you not follow policy?" a defendant chair faces the presumption that he or she was either sloppy or discriminatory.*

more than begging for another chance. By the way, discriminatory application of policy is one of the most common bases of litigation.

Tony had felt pressured both by his colleagues and by Blaine to be supportive in the third-year review. Like many others who felt the force of Blaine's personality, he did not relish being the one to stand up to him, nor did he want to be the one to hurt the man and destroy his career. As Tony eventually realized, he didn't have to stand up to Blaine alone; the people in human relations and the legal office, whom he had bypassed, did it for him.

Bottom line: When drafting correspondence pertaining to anything governed by policy, avoid paraphrasing or summarizing. If you have to summarize for brevity, indicate clearly that what you are providing is only a summary and cite the controlling policy. Also, *always* have everything reviewed and approved. This includes all messages and e-mails dealing with disability, discipline, discrimination, evaluating personnel, hiring and firing, managing grants, promotion and tenure, research management, and any misconduct, including sexual harassment. If you wonder about an issue that is not on this list, get an authoritative opinion.

## ∿ Policy Check ∿

The issues and situations noted in this chapter cover a lot of territory and involve a lot of policy. If you are a chair, it can be daunting to contemplate that you must be familiar with all the rules associated with such problems (yet you will be told this in virtually any book on chairing). The fact is that you may not even wonder about a particular policy until confronted with the very behavior for which it was written. And unfortunately, it may come to you as just that—a confrontation by an angry or frightened member of the faculty demanding your action or a decision. Here's where policy, even if you're ignorant of it, can prove to be your friend. The people on campus who manage and work daily with policy are also your friends; don't fail to capitalize on their experience and willingness to help you.

When that angry or frightened colleague confronts you, listen carefully and clarify to the person's satisfaction that you understand the situation and his or her concern. Then take the wise next step and explain that because the matter is very important to both of you and the stakes may be high, you're going to need some time to look into things and perhaps even do a policy check. Point out that this will protect both of you as well as any others who might be involved.

Taking this step can prove advantageous for several reasons. First, it buys you immediate time that may be needed to collect yourself and for the person confronting you to calm down. Second, it will allow you to engage the right professionals and, with their guidance, to study up on the policy with which you now realize you need to be familiar. You might also be able to collect relevant data, perhaps listen to the other side, and enlist the opinion of trusted colleagues, most notably the dean, the faculty relations officer, and perhaps legal counsel. Finally, and perhaps most important, it prevents you from making a decision that could be hurtful to you and to others, including the institution. Do not procrastinate in following up. The faculty member will be very anxious to hear back from you and could feel that your excuse of checking on policy is merely stalling.

> "I listen to [faculty members] when they have something to get off their chest. I never provide an immediate response but always tell them I'll get back to them in a day or two with an answer to their question or problem. Even if I know what the answer is immediately, I always like to sleep on it to make sure I haven't forgotten about something in my deliberations."
>
> —*Survey comment*

When you say you're going to check on policy, it's OK to admit that you're not fully familiar with the rules. Then, when you meet again, you can say something like "Boy, it's a good thing I checked; we may have to step lightly on this" or "We both appear to have some challenges to face up to." This comes across as both fair and caring, confirming that you have adopted a position of the two of us working together to minimize mistakes and damage, which should help diffuse any anxiety either of you might feel.

Knowing and following policy, or involving people from the legal office, won't guarantee that your problems will be easily solved. When people find themselves in an unfortunate situation, they will look for someone to be responsible, and who could be more convenient than the current chair who is in charge of upholding policy? We've all heard it said that a faculty member who has accepted an administrative assignment has "gone over to the dark side." When a member of the faculty comes up against administration and is "dealt with," it is not uncommon for colleagues to sympathize even if they previously felt the person had it coming—it's classic sympathy for the underdog. Lawsuits have actually occurred with some frequency. If matters turn ugly, think how glad you'll be that you did everything according to policy and followed the counsel of experts.

Two additional steps are essential. First, keep your dean informed and solicit his or her advice and counsel. Second, document everything—carefully. I have found it helpful to send an e-mail to the dean, HR person, or lawyer with whom I have counseled confirming that I have interpreted the person's advice (or the attendant policy) correctly. I also like to have the recipient verify that the step I am about to take is appropriate. It is then wise to both pay attention to and file away the adviser's response; such documentation may prove most helpful later.

If this all sounds heavy, that's because it is. Policy for dealing with important legal issues is formulated to help you navigate treacherous waters, and you should never attempt to ply these waters alone.

## ∿ Policy Exceptions ∿

What if there is no policy for the situation at hand? Can we feel justified in making exceptions?

As our way of doing business changes and technology transforms just about everything we touch, legitimate issues sometimes arise that suggest that a new or modified policy may be in order. It is usually better to look into revising policy that no longer seems to apply rather than repeatedly grant exceptions.

When considering whether to create, change, or grant an exception, keep in mind the "apparent authority" principle. There are a number of factors to consider. Would an exception support the mission of both the department and the institution? Would an exception violate the unit's values? Could it be supported by available resources? Is there a better alternative?

Occasionally people will request an exception to policy just for themselves or their situation. This prompts the question, Would the exception be supported by all who will be affected by it or hear about it? Mary Lou Higgerson and Teddi Joyce point out how little it takes to "create the appearance of favoritism" and that the "best intentions do not guarantee that chairs and deans will be perceived as making fair and equitable decisions."[1]

## ∽ Do You Have Policy on Civility? ∽

Just like Anna and her colleagues in Chapter One, many academics are currently becoming aware of the fact that they do not have policy for dealing with incivility. In a survey just completed on our campus, chairs were asked if their department had a written document that clearly specified performance expectations for faculty. The results revealed that 98 percent had written performance expectations for research, 91 percent for citizenship, 84 percent for teaching, but only 23 percent for civility. Yet problems with civility were prominent among concerns of these same chairs. Darla Twale and Barbara De Luca have observed that our campus is not unique:

> Most, if not all, campuses have a student code of conduct. Has anyone stumbled over a faculty code of conduct anywhere? Probably not. Faculty disciplines and professional areas have codes of ethics that relate only to how research should be conducted and disseminated. Campuses also have policies, procedures, and committees for the proper conduct of research involving human subjects. Actions outside research and publication are unlikely to be formally regulated.[2]

Twale and De Luca recommend that just as with sexual harassment, all institutions should formulate and sanction policy on workplace harassment in general. But, they caution, there is interplay between the two forms of harassment, and the existence of sexual harassment policy may actually encourage incivility.

> The presence of sexual harassment policies and the concomitant sanctions offered to eradicate that problem provided campuses with a false sense of accomplishment for two reasons. First, the underlying problems that caused sexual harassment may also fuel general workplace harassment. However, only one area of harassment was subjected to identification and sanction, and general workplace harassment was overlooked. Second, harassment of a sexual nature is unacceptable, and by default then, other forms of harassment may be acceptable because they were not included in the stated policy.[3]

Robert Cipriano agrees with Twale and De Luca and strongly encourages universities to establish and publish policy and standards for all aspects of civility.[4] His specific suggestions include incorporating civility expectations into the university's mission statement, training faculty on collegiality through human resource workshops, including collegiality as a consideration for promotion and tenure, and in general being proactive about establishing a campus culture that expects, promotes, and rewards civility, collaboration, and peacemaking. When a university has taken such such steps, the chair's ability to correct problem behavior is, of course, greatly enhanced.

# Summary for Step 2: Follow Policy

- Be familiar with campus policies and know where to find them.

- Follow policy scrupulously.

- When working in policy territory, always consult with appropriate professionals.

- Be sure to document all conversations and decisions.

- Consider making exceptions very carefully; keep in mind perceived favoritism and precedent.

## Notes

1. M. L. Higgerson & T. A. Joyce. (2007). *Effective leadership communication: A guide for department chairs and deans for managing difficult situations and people* (p. 37). Bolton, MA: Anker.

2. D. J. Twale & B. M. De Luca. (2008). *Faculty incivility: The rise of the academic bully culture and what to do about it* (p. 156). San Francisco: Jossey-Bass.

3. D. J. Twale & B. M. De Luca. (2008). *Faculty incivility: The rise of the academic bully culture and what to do about it* (p. 153). San Francisco: Jossey-Bass.

4. R. E. Cipriano. (2011). *Facilitating a collegial department in higher education: Strategies for success* (pp. 110–114). San Francisco: Jossey-Bass.

# CHAPTER THREE

# Step 3: Build Trust with Colleagues

## Greg

*Greg, head of the Mathematics Department, sat listening to Sally, an untenured assistant professor who was accusing one of her colleagues of character defamation through a manipulation of e-mail. According to Sally, Roger, another math professor, had sent an e-mail to the chair of the College Curriculum Committee asking about the status of an assignment for which Sally was responsible. Sally had been copied on the message, which pointed out that this was a second request and that the university deadline had passed. The message had also been copied to Greg and to the associate dean.*

*Sally claimed it was the first she had heard of the assignment and that she had never received any previous e-mail about it. She felt it implied that she had been negligent. She had gone to a colleague who was also on the committee and asked to see a copy of Roger's e-mails on the matter. Sure enough, they found that Sally's address was not among the recipients of the first e-mail. The suggestion that she had failed in her duties and that this had been broadcast to her department head and associate dean was distressing to her.*

*This was not the first time Sally had come to Greg with her problems. On several matters she had been quick to blame others. She was a bright mathematician but seemed to have difficulty working through her personal issues. Greg felt frustrated that she was knee deep in yet another issue and might be magnifying it out of proportion. And yet if her perception was accurate, she probably had a legitimate concern.*

What were Greg's options? Here are some that chairs have suggested:

1. He could ask Sally, "What would you like me to do?"
2. He could make sure he understood the situation and Sally's concerns and then offer feedback that reflected her feelings.
3. He could tell Sally to just brush it off and get on with something constructive.
4. He could recommend alternatives for Sally.
5. He could ask Sally, "What alternatives do you see for yourself?"
6. He could check out Sally's story—perhaps contact Roger and see what he had to say.

What did Greg do? He started with option 2—he did what he could to help Sally feel understood. He then chose option 1 and asked her what she wanted him to do. She said she thought that Roger needed to be reprimanded for his deceptiveness. Greg then asked Sally whom she thought should do the reprimanding. She was somewhat dismayed and said, "Why, you, of course." Greg gently pointed out that Roger was her problem, not his. He then asked Sally to explore with him the options that she could pursue to deal with her problem (option 5). She had not spoken with Roger, and doing so soon surfaced as the most logical alternative.

As she stood to leave, Sally became uneasy and asked what she should do if Roger rebuffed her or tried to weasel out of it. Greg then helped her consider a nonaccusatory approach and suggested that if Roger did not receive her to her satisfaction, she could tell him she was going to speak with the department head about it. "But," he told her, "you can come back to me only if you invite him to come with you." Sally paused for a while and then said she would try it.

## ∿ Reflecting on Greg's Options ∿

I chose Greg's case to start the chapter on building trust with colleagues because it is simple and illustrates a fairly common problem, and I believe Greg's actions were effective in building trust. Here's why.

Greg did not own Sally's problem. Sally's problem was with Roger; Greg's problem was with Sally. Greg avoided triangulating, which almost always leads to impaired or injured relationships. Greg noticed that Sally appeared to feel inadequate about confronting Roger; he could have stepped in to assist her. Had he gone to Roger, even to check Roger's side of the story, he might have made enemies out of both Roger and Sally. How so?

First, Sally would have begun viewing Greg as her rescuer, and this would have actually caused her to feel dependent, inadequate, and perhaps victimized. Subconsciously, she would have begrudged Greg for this, even if in the short term she felt appreciative of his intervention. Rather than making Sally dependent, Greg was helping her in a constructive way. He was encouraging her to fend for herself and to develop a skill that she apparently lacked.

Second, Greg avoided making an enemy out of Roger. Even if he had simply asked Roger about the e-mail, it would have been meddling, and Roger, who saw Greg not as just a colleague but as the department head, might have been offended.

Note option 4 that was suggested by some chairs: "He could recommend alternatives for Sally." Greg was wise to avoid directly recommending any alternative, although he did help her see and settle on an option to pursue. Had he proposed a solution that backfired, Sally might have blamed him for that, or if he had suggested an option that worked, Sally would likely have continued to look to him as her problem solver.

After leaving Greg's office, Sally would have started to rethink the matter and weigh whether further pursuit with Roger was worth it. Perhaps she would decide by herself to just brush it off. Note how much better it would be if this were her decision rather than Greg's recommendation.

If Sally did go back and confront Roger, Roger would not have been able to dismiss the issue because Sally had the backup option of returning to Greg. Roger might have preferred to settle the matter with Sally without involving Greg.

If Sally and Roger did return together to Greg's office, Greg would have been able to hear both sides of the matter without independently confronting Roger; he could then more easily maintain balance and fairness. He might have been able to help the two of them work out a resolution.

## ∿ No End Runs ∿

More important than showing that he could be trusted to strengthen his colleagues and not take sides, Greg demonstrated that he did not entertain end runs. When Sally bypassed Roger and took her concern directly to Greg, it not only weakened Sally but also denied Roger a fair hearing. In a case with which I am familiar, a small minority of senior professors made several visits to their dean in an attempt to overturn a decision made by their chair. The dean received them and commiserated with them. When the other faculty, who supported the chair's decision, heard that the dean was not only receiving the protesters but was inviting them back without involving the rest of them *and* without involving the chair, they were appalled.

"These guys bypassed the department because they knew we'd oppose them if they spoke up in-house," they said. "Why does the dean encourage their end runs?"

Needless to say, their trust in and respect for their dean plummeted. How much better things might have been for everyone if the dean had followed Roger's example and helped the minority of senior professors work things out with their colleagues and their chair. We can imagine that they might have complained, "They're not experienced enough" or "He won't listen" or the like. The dean would have been wise to let them know that he was willing to consider their concerns but that he also needed to consider the concerns of everyone in the department. By inviting them to return and bring their chair with them, he would have put a stop to their violation of protocol and also put an immediate hold on their vigilante behavior. The result could have been a stronger department, a stronger chair, and a stronger dean. Chairs should similarly respond to faculty who try to make end runs around program directors or other directors within their departments. They can instead develop a reputation for understanding the issues and then strengthening their colleagues by helping them work things out among themselves.

## ∿ Build Trust with Whom? ∿

When it comes to dealing with problem personnel, there are a number of key people with whom a trusting relationship will prove very important.

### Upper Administration and Campus Experts

Though the circumstances will vary by campus, chairs need to interact with the appropriate professionals when dealing with faculty problems. These could include the director of faculty relations, the people in the equal opportunity office, the administrator in charge of hiring and appointments, the university rank and status officer, the institute's communications or public relations office, and the office of legal counsel. Knowing, befriending, and cooperating with these people is highly recommended; following their policies and direction is essential.

### The Dean

Survey comments were abundant on the importance of the dean as a partner in dealing with problem situations. The most common point was that the dean must be kept informed. "No surprises" was the key message; furthermore, the chair who works closely with the dean benefits from the dean's collegewide perspective, experience, wisdom, and support.

> "I have personally spent time meeting and talking with important staff people in the dean's office, academic affairs, etc. When difficulties arise, that personal relationship has really helped. I spend time getting to know their staff and relate to them on an equal footing."
>
> —*Survey comment*

Here's a tip from a veteran dean: The dean appreciates the chair that comes not with dilemmas but with recommendations, having invested some quality time and best thinking into what might be done. This is not to suggest that a chair should delay sharing a problem or predicament that the dean ought to know about. But much better than "Here's what just happened—what should I do?" is "I thought you ought to know about this; I'll send you my best thinking on it by tomorrow morning." When a chair discovers a problem that the dean ought to know about, the chair should be considerate and diligent enough to think of some options (perhaps by gathering a few wise colleagues to help) and then go to the dean with a proposal or some alternatives to which the dean can react.

## Senior and Respected Colleagues

It is intuitive for a chair to work at building and maintaining trust with the influential members of the department, and much like the dean, not only can these experienced veterans lend their wisdom, but their differing points of view can help the chair keep the nuances of politics and sociology in perspective. Survey comments from chairs included the following:

> "I have a small group of faculty whom I know I can go to and test my ideas. They are trusted colleagues with important experiences."

> "I took over a department that had been through tremendous conflicts and had developed a culture of incivility. Overcoming this has been a real challenge, part of which is made more difficult by the fact that I am the first female department chair. However, I was able to build a coalition that included several very senior males, who disagreed about many things but wanted the climate changed."

> "When dealing with bullying behavior, make sure that the 'senior,' most respected leader in the department gives unequivocal support to the chair. If that unwavering support is not there in the most visible way (e.g., if only lukewarm), . . . it empowers bullies."

When senior colleagues are consulted, it's important that they feel listened to and understood. After conferring with such a group, it would be wise for the chair to say something like this: "Thank you for your input. I will weigh it carefully as I decide how to proceed." This demonstrates that the chair has listened, appreciates the interaction, and owns the responsibility that comes with being the department leader.

## Senate and Union Representatives

Even chairs who perceive that the university senate serves primarily as a forum for discussions or that the union is antagonistic to the interests of administration would do well to get to know the people who represent their faculty, department, and college in these organizations. Getting their perspective, listening to their experiences, and thanking them for the work they do will not only earn their respect but also provide chairs with greater insight as to what has worked well and what hasn't when dealing with personnel issues at their institution.

## Staff and Support Personnel

The people working in staff and support roles characteristically constitute the most stable component of the workforce at a college or university. Without them, there would be no plumbing, electricity, food services, or even paychecks. They develop strong networks that are often independent of departments or academic boundaries and gain tremendous insight into the workings that support the institution. Perhaps most important, they persist in their key roles while students, chairs, deans, provosts, and presidents come and go. It is essential that the chair interact with these strategic people, acknowledging them, seeking their advice, and looking after their interests, thereby earning both their favor and their trust.

## The Person Who Is Perceived to Be the Problem

Building trust with a challenging colleague rather than marginalizing the person may be difficult and even feel inappropriate, especially if the challenging colleague has not behaved in a way that invites trust. Some steps that a chair can take to build trust with the challenging colleague (and all other colleagues as well) are discussed here. Note that I recommend these points as something that *you*, as chair, should look to implement within *yourself*; be slow to view these as behavioral expectations of others.

## ∿ Build Trust How? ∿

Trust is a fascinating attribute. We earn or generate it through our own effort, yet with the exception of trusting in ourselves, we cannot draw on or collect the trust we generate until it is given or extended to us by someone else. In other words, we build our trust accounts outside of ourselves. Chairs are in an ideal position to build colleague-held trust accounts. Here are some ways to do it.

## Start by Extending Trust

"Let go; trust those you trust," wrote a survey respondent. I had a personal experience that confirmed the validity of that suggestion. Our family was living in Morocco. At the height of the orange season, I was driving in a part of Rabat where I had never been before. As I was passing a small fruit stand, I spotted some particularly beautiful oranges. I stopped and sampled one and decided to buy two cases. After they were loaded into my car, I found that I had no cash. The shopkeeper, who had never seen me before, put his hand on mine and said, "No problem. You pay me later." I felt a powerful obligation to pay that debt—primarily because trust had been extended to me when I hadn't earned it. I returned to the fruit stand the next day and paid the man. After that I often went out of my way to drive to that little fruit stand.

Granted, I had never been a problem to the orange merchant; he had not interacted with me over a period of time and found me challenging. Extending trust to me was relatively easy for him. If distrust between us had developed over the years, it would have been unreasonable for him to simply touch my hand and say, "No problem." Where there's a history of difficulty, patience is required. However, consider the power of extending trust and also how much easier it is for a chair to do it than it is for the faculty member who feels marginalized. With the benefit of relatively more power and authority, a chair is actually derelict if he or she fails to capitalize on that position and make the first move.

## Trust but Verify

To trust you must also verify. There are many sides to every story, and it's crucial to a leader's credibility that, like a good reporter, the leader verify the story before believing it or publishing it. What is the other side of the matter? What is the source? Was there a second witness? One may never be able to tease out the complete truth on issues where humans are involved because perceptions, attitudes, and emotions vary widely. An emotional truth may not be acceptable to others, but it represents reality for the person embracing it. Leaders must be diligent in searching out both factual and emotional truths and should postpone their trust in any situation where there is misgiving or uncertainty.

## Be Open and Transparent

"Don't expect that the department has to trust you on something without sharing as much of the background information as possible," one survey respondent advised.

In response to the question "What has helped you be a better chair?" hundreds of survey respondents volunteered "be open" and "be transparent." An important way to be transparent is to allow people at all levels to see and hear the concern you have for the self-worth of everyone in your unit, including those who are viewed as problematic. The chair who shows that he or she cares about colleagues enough to be completely honest with them will enjoy their allegiance and commitment.

Transparency takes courage. It can be risky to remove our facade and expose our tender underbelly. There is fear that doing so will lead to a loss of standing or respect. Patrick Lencioni writes, however, that trust is the first essential component of a functional team and that genuine trust exists among colleagues only when they are "comfortable being vulnerable with one another." He notes that trust-through-transparency people "admit weaknesses and mistakes, ask for help, accept questions and input about their areas of responsibility, and offer and accept apologies without hesitation."[1] The chair should lead the way, and a good way to encourage this kind of transparency in others is to get to know them personally and discover their interests.

As you consider the interests of all players, including the interests of the challenging colleague, be aware that some interests may be the same as yours and some may be quite different. Be open about this and discuss it with those involved. Also, make sure (and make public) that your key personal interests are aligned with those of the department and the institution.

As discussed in Chapter One, it is important to revisit and communicate openly about the mission and values that the department has laid down for itself. People trust others who share their values, and departments that frequently revisit and discuss their unifying standards enjoy healthy levels of trust.

Bring sensitive issues into the open, explain things, and answer questions as best you can. It is unwise to ignore something that everyone knows about and is being whispered in the hallways. If you have data or documents, seek legal counsel before sharing, but then be open with what is approved for disclosure. If you are unable to share any information, explain that it is because of confidentiality or legal concerns; never say simply "no comment."

If you don't know something, admit it; don't bluff. Confessing ignorance on any issue invariably ends up making you look better than pretending you know something you don't. When someone is discussing a problem situation or person with you, always ask for clarification if you have any doubt about the story or its meaning. This often avoids serious misunderstandings later.

Finally, openness must be protected with tact and consideration. As you become aware of a problem with a colleague's performance, be thoughtful enough to share your perception with that person first, not with others. Disclose your intentions and your objectives. To do this you might say, "I may have insufficient information, so I'm open to feedback. Let me share what I've observed (or heard), and then I want to listen to you." By being honest and showing consideration, you help others trust you and therefore also help them be open themselves— not only to what is bothering them but also to what might be done to alleviate the problem.

## Never Put Down People or Policy

"As to potential conflicts," one survey respondent noted, "I have one policy: 'Don't say it in public or even in private if you can't say it to the individual.' It is amazing how that helps to level the playing field."

When you speak or write about someone who is absent (even if the person may never learn about what you say or write), make every effort to do so with wording that you would be willing to have that person see or hear. That way, the persons who do hear you know that they can trust you to speak well of them in their absence too. When communicating about a challenging colleague or problem situation, limit your language to unembellished facts—especially if done in writing. Avoid absolutist statements; temper those points with qualifiers by writing "*perceived* misconduct," "*apparent* lack of motivation," and so on.

Never approve or wink at anything that is contrary to university policy or to the directives of those in authority; otherwise your trust is immediately compromised.

## Keep Confidences

Keeping confidences is crucial to maintaining trust, but it can be difficult. I have found the following advice helpful.

Be prepared to say, "I'm sorry; that's confidential, and I'm committed to honoring the confidence."

If someone pumps you for confidential information about someone else, say, "I understand that you feel it is important for you to know about this; I suggest you speak with X directly."

If approaching X is inappropriate, say, "To be fair both to X and to you, I'm keeping this matter confidential. I believe X would not appreciate its being discussed, and I don't want to put you in the difficult situation of having to watch what you say. The best of us can accidentally let something slip."

If someone shares information that you think should have been kept confidential, say, "I'm not comfortable with this information. It feels like something that should be kept confidential, and now I have the burden of remembering not to talk about it. I don't believe I can make constructive use of this. If there's any more, I'd prefer to be kept in the dark."

## Don't Ignore Troubling Behavior

Troubling behavior even of a moderate order, if left unattended long enough, will erode not only trust but also morale. Consider the faculty member who plateaued several years ago and whose competence has become outdated. Or there's the person who is constantly negative, even if only slightly, but enough to disturb all those who work with her. Perhaps someone is too energetic and steamrolls his colleagues as he pursues his own agenda at their expense. Tips on how to interact with these and other types of disturbing colleagues are provided in Chapter Six and in Part Two, but it should be pointed out here that when colleagues see that problem behavior is allowed to persist unchecked over years, they lose their trust in the system and in the chair for not stepping up and effecting a change.

## Don't Go It Alone

Even the smartest veteran chair with many battle scars cannot succeed without the assistance and trust of others. As James Watson, the Nobel Prize–winning scientist, observed, "If you're the brightest person in the room, you're in trouble."[2] His point is that people who are experienced often try to handle things alone rather than involving helpers. A condition that Robert Cialdini calls "captainitis" occurs when a chair attempts to go it alone, resulting in the equally regrettable tendency of the rest of the faculty to simply stand by and watch, shirking their responsibility and thus weakening not just themselves but the entire department.[3]

Ron Heifetz put it well:

> The lone-warrior model of leadership is heroic suicide. Each of us has blind spots that require the vision of others. Each of us has passions that need to be contained by others. Anyone can lose the capacity to get on the balcony, particularly when the pressures mount. Every person who leads needs help in distinguishing self from role and identifying the underlying issues that generate attack.[4]

This is not to suggest that a chair ought to expect the dean, HR, or a committee of trusted peers to take on the responsibility of interacting with challenging colleagues but rather that the chair who solicits and weighs the counsel of colleagues and associates not only earns more of their trust but is also much better able to make a sound decision and enjoy support from multiple directions when any action is taken.

*"The lone-warrior model of leadership is heroic suicide."*

# Summary for Step 3: Build Trust with Colleagues

- Don't accommodate or encourage end runs.

- Be the first to extend trust, even to those who don't deserve it.

- Be open and show concern for others.

- Never put down people or policy.

- Keep confidences.

- Don't ignore problematic behavior.

## Notes

1. P. Lencioni. (2002). *The Five Dysfunctions of a Team: A Leadership Fable* (pp. 195, 197). San Francisco: Jossey-Bass.

2. M. Lemonick. (2003, February 17). James Watson: "You have to be obsessive." *Time.* Retrieved from http://www.time.com/time /magazine/article/0,9171,1004245,00.html

3. R. B. Cialdini. (2004). The perils of being the best and the brightest. *Harvard Management Communication Letter, 1*(2), 3–5.

4. R. A. Heifetz. (1994). *Leadership without easy answers* (p. 268). Cambridge, MA: Harvard University Press.

# CHAPTER FOUR

# Step 4: Evaluate Yourself and Your Perceptions

## Darby

*Darby was only ten minutes into his lecture when he noticed that one of his students had fallen asleep. He tried to ignore this, but the student was sprawled over the edge of his desk and had started to snore. His shirt had ridden up above his belt to expose a hairy belly button. Embarrassed by this distraction, which reflected on his teaching, Darby turned and erased a formula from the chalkboard. When he'd finished, he hefted the spongy eraser in his hand, then turned back to the class and swiftly propelled it at the sleeping student; it struck him on the shoulder and bounced high into the dust-filled air.*

*No one laughed.*

*"I'm sorry," the student stammered as he gathered himself and sat up.*

*Darby felt heat in his ears and found it hard to focus for the rest of the class; it was as if a bowl had closed in around him and he had difficulty thinking beyond its perimeter to what he had planned to do next.*

> *Students departed quickly when the bell rang. The remaining three weeks of the semester didn't go well. Darby had been teaching for thirty-five years. Now he was unsure of himself in a way he had never experienced before. He remained angry at that student until he retired.*

Upon reading this story, what do you feel? Can you empathize with Darby? Do you judge him disapprovingly? The story is true; I was a junior colleague of Darby's and heard about the chalkbrush story both from Darby and from some of the students. It was well known that Darby's lectures were boring at times. Although I disapprove of what he did, I can relate to how he felt and am relieved that I was not the one who threw the eraser. The incident came back to me as I was researching materials for this book and read something written by the Arbinger Institute:

> The other guy's a jerk! But remember ... I actually *need* the other guy to keep being a jerk so that I'll remain justified in blaming him for being a jerk.[1]

I can guess that Darby stayed angry for the rest of the semester, and even years later, to justify having thrown that eraser. Had Darby's chair learned about the incident just after it happened, what might the chair have done? Perhaps he would have just laughed about it, but would he have had any success in asking Darby to consider making reparation? Might he have advised Darby to put more spark into his lectures or helped him come up with opportunities for interactivity or group discussions? Perhaps the more important question is, had the chair suggested any of a number of options to Darby, would Darby have accepted them? Here's more from Arbinger:

> Identify someone with a problem and you'll be identifying someone who resists the suggestion that he has a problem. That's self-deception—the inability to see that one has a problem. Of all the problems in organizations, it's the most common—and the most damaging.[2]

It's very likely that Darby would have resisted the suggestion that the cause of his lingering anger was his own poor teaching skills. It would be easier to go on deceiving himself into believing that it was the sleeping student that had spoiled his class. Consider someone's behavior that vexes us. Others can see it, but they appear to be blind to it or at least indifferent. We begin thinking, "If only they could be helped to see and accept their status as department albatross! If they could change their ways, it would make life more productive and more enjoyable for all of us."

This is when self-deception becomes most operative and perhaps most alarming. The "someone with a problem" could well be us, not them. We too could be like Darby. We could resist the suggestion that we have a problem—a problem with how we view our colleague—thinking that all would be well if only the other person would change. Focusing on the behavior that irritates us can be our proof that the other guy is a jerk. We might actually begin to hope the twit will do yet one more thing that exasperates us so that we can look knowingly at one of our colleagues and even take pleasure in gossiping about it.

*The "someone with a problem" could well be us, not them.*

This takes us back, as chairs, to the important question asked in the Introduction: "How should a chair view the challenge of problem faculty?" Do we really want to work with our challenging colleagues, or do we want to bemoan them, castigate them, and take spiteful pleasure in complaining about them? Are we so biased against them that we're unable to even consider that our own perceptions and reactions to those perceptions are a major part of the problem?

## ∿ Unloading Our Prejudices ∿

It's not easy to let go of our prejudices. Oxford University professor C. S. Lewis wrote about a man who had ridden a bus to the edge of paradise and was shown what the place was like.[3] He was told that he could enter paradise if he would remove his prejudice, leave it at the side of the road, and walk in. The man took off his bundle of bigotry and began to walk. Then he stopped, hesitated, and went back. He didn't feel like himself without his burden; there was a conspicuous void. His prejudice was an essential part of him—he had built and nurtured and sustained it for most of his life. He stooped and picked up his prejudice, positioned it comfortably on his shoulders, and got back on the bus.

Now, to have someone suggest that in order to modify the behavior of a colleague or to mend a flawed system created and sustained by others, we must start by changing ourselves can feel like an insult. The easiest way for our problem faculty troubles to go away would of course be for the problem people to either change or be tossed out. Looking for an external solution or a technician to fix things is much preferred. Ron Heifetz notes that "even the toughest individual tends to avoid realities that require adaptive work, searching instead for an authority, a physician, to provide the way out."[4]

As many chairs attest, however, when confronted with some of the harsher realities of personnel problems, there is great wisdom in looking first to change ourselves if we hope to be successful and enjoy the journey. Consider a challenging-faculty situation of your own that appears intractable. Now view it in light of how you might modify your own perception and behavior—even if it's only how you talk about it to others. Can you begin to feel at least an element of manageability? Doesn't deciding to change how you view the problem actually give you some measure of control over it, at least by modifying the degree to which you let it bother you?

> "People are fundamentally the same everywhere and they have been that way forever. This includes pettiness, backstabbing, fomenting conspiracies, etc., as well as the higher attributes typically associated with educators. Therefore, the only significant changes one can expect as chair or director are within you. Find knowledgeable and mature confidants with whom to speak about challenges—but know that you can't change the wind; you can only change your sails. (Not my maxim, of course.)"
>
> —*Survey comment*

Stephen Covey writes, "No one can persuade another to change. Each of us guards a gate of change that can only be opened from the inside. We cannot open the gate of another, either by argument or by emotional appeal."[5] He goes on to say that when we decide to open our own gate of change, our growth can be evolutionary and the net effect can be revolutionary. He further states: "Anytime we think the problem is 'out there,' that thought is the problem. We empower what's out there to control us."[6]

Although it can feel like retreating from the issue, like wimping out, especially when a colleague has just acted like a certified jerk or has fallen short of a responsibility yet one more time, stopping to ask ourselves to what extent we are responsible for the disappointment can be powerful. It's not instinctive, and it's not easy. Like Darby, who threw the chalkbrush, or the man who was uncomfortable unloading his prejudice at the edge of paradise, we all find it difficult to adjust to the notion that things could be better if we would make a change in ourselves. But if we make an honest attempt, an internal transformation can come quickly.

Here are three questions that chairs might ask themselves to help minimize internal prejudice with respect to a challenging colleague:

- What are this colleague's anxieties, trials, burdens, and pains?
- How am I, or our department, adding to their problems?
- In what ways have we neglected or mistreated this colleague?

Veteran chair and former dean Deryl Leaming writes:

We often forget that our colleagues may not have others in whom they can confide. Can you make it comfortable for them to share some of the personal things in their life that trouble them? Do you want to play that role? If you can, and are willing to accept that as a part of your responsibility as chairperson, you may be able to help, but not everyone is able to make this "beyond the job" commitment.[7]

## ◡ Being "Quick to Observe" ◡

As we ask ourselves the kinds of questions listed previously it is essential that we pay attention to what we feel. If we really want to make things better, it is very likely that we'll be prompted to take some action. Former dean and university president David Bednar addresses this in his concept of being "quick to observe." He notes that the word *observe* has two meanings: "notice" and "obey."[8] If we are quick to observe, we will be on the lookout for signs of what we should do, and once we notice those signs, we will be quick to act on (obey) the feelings that accompany our observation.

Bednar's concept can be quickly illustrated by a man driving a car. When he leaves the freeway and heads off onto a rural road, he may wonder what the speed limit now is. If he's attentive, he'll be quick to observe (notice) the familiar black-and-white rectangle that says "55 MPH" as soon as it appears.

When the driver observes (sees) the speed limit sign, an important issue will be whether he observes (obeys) it. Step two of Bednar's "be quick to observe" is to obey the prompts that come to us when we notice something. Chairs who are looking for signs that colleagues are struggling will notice them, and if they are perceptive, these chairs will also sense ways that they can help alleviate the struggles. What might they do for a problem person in a service capacity? How could the person's dilemma become the chair's dilemma? How could the chair reach out to help? Ask for a reprint of a recent article? Attend and share a positive comment about the person's performance? Engage the colleague in a conversation in which the chair practices careful listening? How about sending a personal handwritten note?

Academic chairs are in an ideal position to be watching for signs. They're expected to be paying attention to everyone; it's their charge. They have access to personnel files; they monitor performance and circumstances; they set or recommend salary adjustments. To fail to be quick to observe signs of stress, withdrawal, or resentment or to spot eagerness to be involved would be derelict. "If we are observant," Leaming says, "we may find signals that tell us there is more troubling the faculty member than he or she is telling us. Lack of good eye contact might be one such signal."[9]

If a chair has built some rapport, some acceptance, some trust, there's a better chance for corrective interaction to be successful. Bednar says that if we practice being quick to observe (both noticing and obeying what we feel), we will develop discernment. In other words, we will enhance our perception, insight, and understanding. Here's a scenario:

> As you leave the office to go home, you notice through a partly open door one of your colleagues sitting at his desk; he does not look up at the sound of your steps. As you walk down the hall, you reflect on the fact that he seems to have been disengaged lately, sort of withdrawn. You think about going back to ask how he's doing.

What happens if you ignore the prompt to go back? Well, first of all, if this man is hurting in some way and you don't reach out to him, you will have failed him. And second, something happens to you; your ability to discern the needs of others atrophies. Think of someone you know who is great at spotting the person in need and who seems to know just how to approach the person—what to say and what to do. Being quick at both noticing how others appear to be feeling and then quickly obeying the impulse to interact in the appropriate way very likely accounts for this skill. Quickness to observe in both ways is what such perceptive folks have practiced, and because of that practice, they have developed strength of discernment, of knowing what to say and do.

Returning to the matter of unloading our prejudices, it may be that when we observe a colleague in distress, our response will at first be no more than to revisit the way we feel about about the person, realizing that no matter how thorny the situation may seem, there really is something we can do, even if it's only to modify our outlook. And once our outlook is modified, ways often open up for us to be helpful.

> *No matter how thorny the situation may seem, there really is something we can do, even if it's only to modify our outlook.*

## ∿ Setbacks ∿

When attempting to modify our outlook, we should expect setbacks. First of all, whenever we engage in any form of self-change, especially if we've not tried it before, we usually realize that it isn't easy—we're out of practice. Professor Will Winder is an exercise physiologist; he's an expert on getting and staying in physical shape. He says that fitness has a half-life of about a week. That is, if a fit person abruptly stops exercising and becomes completely sedentary, as when consigned to bed rest, the person's muscles lose about half of their energy-supplying capacity in just seven days. After only two weeks of being completely sedentary, only 25 percent of the former muscle power is left.

Will's research on reverse half-life, or getting back into shape, is perhaps more discouraging. If someone wanted to double the energy-supplying capacity of muscles in one week, the person would need to exercise strenuously for two hours a day, five days a week. "Of course, the completely sedentary person could not do that," Will explained. "There are other physiological adjustments involved, notably the status of the heart."[10] It's interesting that Will mentioned the heart first. Having our heart right is essential for effective physical exercise as well as effective interactions with people. Someone has said, "There are two things that will stress the heart: running up stairs and running down people." Will says it usually takes months to get a heart in shape after a prolonged sedentary interlude. So if we've been completely sedentary with respect to being quick to notice and respond to the needs of others, we should be prepared to struggle for some time before we're even moderately good at it.

Also, as we think about getting our heart right toward that challenging member of the faculty we must be especially careful that, knowing the importance of the heart, we don't focus on whether the other person's heart is right toward us or toward anyone else. We can only get our own heart right; we achieve nothing by fussing over the status of someone else's heart.

> *We can only get our own heart right; we achieve nothing by fussing over the status of someone else's heart.*

Finally, that problem colleague may bristle at our overture, and if that happens, we will be inclined to say to ourselves, "See, there's the proof that this character really is a jerk!" If we stoop to that perception, it will be easier to place all blame on the other party, to stop trying to get our heart right, and to take a little "bed rest" where we can atrophy in avoidance, criticism, and blaming.

Speaking of bristling, there's an important concept to keep in mind when dealing with people who become agitated, even hostile or violent. People in such a state are actually temporarily handicapped. Research indicates that when we're highly aroused, we literally start to go blind.[11] Our peripheral vision virtually disappears, and we focus only on what's immediately in front of us. Understandably, we also lose the ability to hear what others are saying (peripheral hearing is lost), and instead we focus only on what we want to say. Malcolm Gladwell writes that people become briefly autistic when their emotions are cranked up. "Arousal leaves us mind blind," he says, and we're unable to see, let alone process, the social signals that would otherwise be available to us.[12]

## ∿ Lizard Brain ∿

The expression "lizard brain" has been used to describe our mental condition when we lose our composure, when the higher-order functions of our brain are shut off, leaving us with only our basic motor skills, including fight or flight. It may actually take days for us to recover completely from this state. Unfortunately, pride sometimes denies us a release from lizard thinking toward someone for years or even a lifetime.

When someone goes lizard on us, it's important to recognize what has happened and to cut the person a little slack. That was not the real Darby who threw the chalkbrush. That was semi-reptile Darby, whose brain had been commandeered by his emotions. The real Darby, the warm Darby, the likable Darby—even if he was a little boring at times—almost always prevailed.

And of course, it's not just other people; we too may go lizard at times. If you're prone to going lizard and resolve to not do it today, be aware that your unconscious attitudes may override the values you espouse and that emotion can easily commandeer your rationality. Once we recognize it for what it is—a temporary state of blaming others for not only our strong feelings but also our embarrassing behavior—we can call on the higher-order capacity of our frontal cortex and tap in to our better emotional pools and do at least two things: forgive ourselves and craft an apology to the other person. "This is the real me speaking now" will be our message. "The lizard in me took over yesterday, and I behaved badly." Such apologies usually work in two ways: first, we feel better, and second, we recover from the incident quickly.

> "Wait for at least 24 hours to 'cool off' before having discussions that could lead to a possible very negative outcome. Gather as much information as possible before positive or negative discussions."
>
> —*Survey comment*

Keep in mind that there are times when it's absolutely appropriate to go lizard. When you feel yourself in danger, go ahead and act like a reptile—but choose flight rather than fight; leave and get help. Tell security or the dean or human resources what happened. Never try to deal with a dangerous situation by yourself. It's OK to say that you need to take a break to calm down, but get yourself out. As the authors of *Crucial Confrontations* put it:

> Your grandmother was wrong when she counseled you on the eve of your wedding never to go to bed angry. When you're angry, going to bed may be exactly the thing you need to dissipate your adrenaline, regain your brainpower, and prepare to return to the confrontation.[13]

## ∿ An Optimistic Note ∿

Here's an encouraging observation: If you've read this far, you're apparently willing to work on your people skills and practice at succeeding with challenging colleagues. Others are looking for a quick fix; you know better. You understand what it takes to be fit. In fact, you've probably been exercising and practicing already.

The authors of *Influencer: The Power to Change Anything* cite the lifework of noted psychologist Anders Ericsson, who concludes that gifted people do not inherit their gifts; they become exceptional through deliberate practice. Ericsson notes that Olympic-hopeful figure skaters practice differently from other skaters.

> Olympic hopefuls work on skills they yet have to master. Club skaters, in contrast, work on skills they've already mastered. Amateurs tend to spend *half* of their time at the rink chatting with friends and not practicing at all.[14]

These authors then make a point that is particularly germane to our interest in problem faculty and interpersonal skills:

> The fact that improvements in performance come through deliberate practice makes all the sense in the world when it comes to activities such as figure skating, playing chess, and mastering the violin.... Most of us don't even think that soft and gushy interpersonal skills are something you need to study at all, let alone something you'd study and practice.[15]

So if we want to be effective at interacting productively with challenging colleagues, we'll need to practice, probably a lot. We'll work at identifying, letting go of, and then

*Most of us don't think that interpersonal skills are something we need to study and practice.*

becoming comfortable without our long-held prejudices. We'll discard our derogatory labels for others. We'll discipline ourselves to focus on what we can do to change ourselves. We won't atrophy in bed rest. We'll work to get *our* heart in shape—and not worry about theirs.

If this all sounds too soft, too gentle and impractical, too much like accommodating or even encouraging the sluggard or tyrant in your midst, don't give up reading yet. Taking effective action is addressed in Chapter Six, where we'll consider how to be suitably tough when it's warranted.

## Summary for Step 4: Evaluate Yourself and Your Perceptions

- Be slow to label others as problems.

- Evaluate your prejudices, and make appropriate changes within yourself.

- Ask thoughtful questions about what might be causing challenging behaviors.

- Be quick to observe (notice *and* obey) what you feel you should do.

- Practice, practice, practice the interpersonal skills you're not good at.

### Notes

1. Arbinger Institute. (2006). *The anatomy of peace: Resolving the heart of conflict* (p. 153). San Francisco: Berrett-Koehler.

2. Arbinger Institute. (2006). *The anatomy of peace: Resolving the heart of conflict* (p. 16). San Francisco: Berrett-Koehler.

3. C. S. Lewis. (2001). *The great divorce: A dream.* San Francisco: HarperCollins. (Original work published 1946)

4. R. A. Heifetz. (1994). *Leadership without easy answers* (p. 76). Cambridge, MA: Harvard University Press.

5. S. R. Covey. (1989). *The seven habits of highly effective people: Restoring the character ethic* (pp. 60–61). New York: Simon & Schuster.

6. S. R. Covey. (1989). *The seven habits of highly effective people: Restoring the character ethic* (p. 89). New York: Simon & Schuster.

7. D. R. Leaming. (2007). *Academic leadership: A practical guide to chairing the department* (2nd ed., p. 364). Bolton, MA: Anker.

8. D. A. Bednar. (2005). "Quick to observe." In *Speeches (Brigham Young University), 2005–2006* (pp. 15–24). Provo, UT: BYU Publications and Graphics.

9. D. R. Leaming. (2007). *Academic leadership: A practical guide to chairing the department* (2nd ed., p. 337). Bolton, MA: Anker.

10. W. Winder, personal communication, July 2011.

11. K. Patterson, J. Grenny, R. McMillan, & A. Switzler. (2002). *Crucial conversations: Tools for talking when stakes are high* (p. 50). New York: McGraw-Hill.

12. M. Gladwell. (2005). *Blink: The power of thinking without thinking* (pp. 221–226). New York: Little, Brown.

13. K. Patterson, J. Grenny, R. McMillan, & A. Switzler. (2005). *Crucial confrontations: Tools for resolving broken promises, violated expectations, and bad behavior* (p. 195). New York: McGraw-Hill.

14. K. Patterson, J. Grenny, D. Maxfield, R. McMillan, & A. Switzler. (2008). *Influencer: The power to change anything* (p. 118). New York: McGraw-Hill.

15. K. Patterson, J. Grenny, D. Maxfield, R. McMillan, & A. Switzler. (2008). *Influencer: The power to change anything* (p. 119). New York: McGraw-Hill.

# CHAPTER FIVE

# Step 5: Listen

## Charlie

*Charlie was the new chair of the Biology Department. Paulo was a full professor and had been in the department longer than anyone. He dressed impeccably, and his speech and manners were refined. Charlie had just stepped into Paulo's office. It was going to be their first real conversation; they had previously only exchanged greetings or spoken briefly to each other in faculty meetings. Charlie had actually avoided Paulo over the years, feeling that the little man was a bit of an oddball, but as chair, he was concerned about a decline that he had noted in Paulo's productivity over the past three years. Paulo seemed to be even more reclusive, and there was a report that he had recently sworn at a visiting postdoc who had been using the microtome in his lab. It seemed so uncharacteristic.*

*Their conversation was polite but shallow as Charlie showed interest in the collection of lichens Paulo had on his shelves. When they sat down, Charlie wasn't sure how to transition into the subject of Paulo's productivity, and almost*

> *without thinking, he said, "So what was the deal about Arthur and the microtome?"*
>
> *Paulo immediately stood up and pointed his finger at Charlie. "I knew that was what this was about," he said. "You come in here pretending to be paying a friendly visit, and ... You get out of my office," he hissed. "Get out now, do you hear?" He moved from behind his desk and walked toward the door.*

What should Charlie do? At this moment his prudent options essentially boil down to two: he can exit Paulo's office, or he can stay seated and attempt reconciliation. If he leaves, there will remain a huge chasm between the two of them, and bridging it later will be difficult. If he stays, it could constitute a direct challenge to Paulo.

If Charlie gets up and leaves, he might do so feeling that Paulo is a jerk and consider Paulo's outburst as one more reason to justify thinking of him that way. Or he might realize that he shouldn't have confronted Paulo about the microtome right off and would spend days trying to find a comfortable way to restart the conversation. Is declining Paulo's order to leave an option? Paulo is conspicuously exercised; something deep inside him has been triggered. Would it be better just to get out of his way or to attempt to uncover what is eating at him? If he does try to stay, what could Charlie say?

Actually, the key does not lie in what Charlie says but rather in how he feels. If he truly wants to understand Paulo and wants to attend to Paulo's best interests, he will signal with his eyes, his facial expressions, his posture, and his vocal tones that he cares about Paulo. Of course, the fact that he so quickly asked about the microtome suggests that he didn't intend to try to understand Paulo, even though he may have thought he did. Given Paulo's response, any attempt at on-the-spot repair may not be possible.

If, prior to entering Paulo's office, Charlie had reflected on the importance of their initial meeting, on the significance of his new role as chair and how he was perceiving himself as well as how he was apt to be perceived by Paulo, or on how little he knew about Paulo and the indication that something had apparently gone wrong in the man's life recently, he would probably have resolved to do nothing more in his first visit than express an interest in Paulo and help him feel appreciated. If this had been his plan, he would probably not have mentioned the microtome.

## ∿ Caring ∿

The key to effective listening lies in caring about the other person—and caring deeply enough that we let go of our own need to be heard and focus instead on helping the other person feel understood. When someone has misbehaved or when there's a distance between us, as there was between Charlie and Paulo, it can take great effort to shove aside our self-centered agenda and focus on the other person, on discovering what he or she is feeling and why.

Several years ago Ann Lucas interviewed one hundred chairs and asked them to identify characteristics of difficult colleagues.[1] Their descriptions included lagging performance, limited interaction, using sarcasm, avoiding responsibility, denigrating students, and poor scholarship. Lucas

*The key to effective listening lies in caring about the other person.*

then interviewed twenty-five of those who were so described. She found that "the most frequent explanation they offered for their current feelings and behaviors was that they had been treated unjustly by chairs and administrators." Some felt unappreciated for work they had done or struggled with a loss of previous influence or power. Some were burdened with a personal issue such as a death, a prolonged illness, a wayward child, or a personal addiction. Lucas reports that the alienated people "were usually very willing to talk about their own plight. They generally felt very isolated in the department. There was no one with whom they could even have a cup of coffee or go to lunch."

Neuroscience researchers have determined that when people feel isolated, they register the same brain response as when they experience physical pain, particularly in the region where suffering is registered.[2] Suffering draws oxygen and energy away from productivity, with the result that performance lags.

Lucas reported that most of the chairs in her study did not know how to help their alienated colleagues. Her first recommendation was to simply reach out to them on a human level, warming up to them a few times, stopping by their office to engage in small talk, and after a few weeks perhaps requesting their assistance or advice on some matter. She says this kind of interaction could provide an opening for the chair to say, "I have missed your active involvement in the department. What would it take to bring you back into the mainstream?"

Even after a preparatory warmup, the person may respond with a tirade once the matter of his or her performance is brought up. If this happens, Lucas says that the chair should not react or respond defensively but should just listen. "Having someone listen to you and understand your point of view is very affirming," she writes, "and difficult or abrasive colleagues get little affirmation." She reports that in her research, chairs that have tried warming up to and finding ways to involve a challenging faculty member have had a 92 percent success rate, which she defines as "the chair's having a better relationship with the difficult faculty member, the individual's getting more involved or accepting more responsibility in the department, and the individual's making fewer abrasive comments in meetings."

Tom Fiutak is an international expert on managing conflict; he says that when people begin to cry and swear, rather than retreating in panic or withdrawing into the disquieting safety of false peace, we should celebrate that the issue is finally out in the open where we can deal with it and not leave it hidden, smoldering, while we and others pretend it doesn't exist or feel bewildered or embarrassed about the outburst.[3]

Had Charlie taken as long as several months to warm up to Paulo, it's possible that Paulo would have shared an agitation, a hurt, or a fear, even if it weren't the one that bothered him the most, just to see how Charlie would respond. And even if Paulo never did bring up anything substantive, Charlie would have been establishing a relationship and hence would have earned the right to gently confront Paulo with the fact that the records indicated a slump in his productivity and ask what the department could do to help. Listening, carefully, all the while trying to understand what made his eccentric colleague tick would be Charlie's objective because his goal would be to rehabilitate Paulo, restore him to his former level of productivity, and better assimilate him and his talents into the department.

As he did this, Charlie would likely have learned much more from what Paulo did than from what he said. Just as "show, don't tell" is one of the basic rules of good writing, listening experts tell us that we can usually listen better with our eyes than with our ears. What events does Paulo attend or miss? Where does he sit? With whom does he talk? What do his facial expressions and body language reveal? Making such observations would constitute powerful listening if Charlie were "quick to observe." Not only would Charlie want to notice how Paulo acted and what signals he was sending, but he would also want to obey the prompts that Charlie felt within himself regarding what he might do to earn the permission to be able to speak more openly with Paulo. Of course, there would be no progress made toward department improvement if Charlie simply focused on what an oddball Paulo was.

This kind of observing and responding to what we perceive is useful when interacting with the spectrum of problem faculty characters in our midst. One might be the person who is scraping by doing the bare minimum—apparently waiting until enough years have been put in to retire with full benefits. Another might be the one who receives bad teaching scores but insists that the students in this generation are spoiled and haven't ever experienced the realities of failure as a consequence of not working hard. It probably wouldn't work very well to confront either of these persons directly with a reprimand. By looking into the specifics of their activities, how they spend their time, what things they do well, and comments they make in meetings and by going out of our way to get to know them on a personal level and getting at their story, we will almost certainly earn their trust as well as notice something that we can do—if not directly to help, at least to describe more effectively the gap we notice between their performance and what is expected of them. We can then explore with them what it would take to erase that disparity.

## ∿ The Buttoned Lip ∿

Commented one survey respondent, "Listen but don't immediately come up with a solution, even if you have one in mind."

Perhaps our biggest listening challenge is to avoid the strong desire to talk. Deryl Leaming says, "When we listen to complaints, we are tempted to engage in conversation, to respond with logical arguments and/or solutions, to judge, or to criticize. Generally, it is better to listen silently, doing little more than showing concerned interest."[4]

Kerry Patterson and colleagues agree.[5] They write that when we're dealing with problematic people, we're not likely to get very far with verbal arguments. While we're trying to convince other people that we're right and they're wrong, they're not listening at all except to find errors in our logic or mistakes in our facts and to prepare counterarguments. Of course, if we're both doing the same thing, our net progress toward reaching a solution will probably be negative.

Although it can help to rehearse or even memorize some key words or terms to use before we confront someone who may not want to talk to us, we need to be careful. This tactic can come off as mechanical and phony and thus backfire. The key is to focus on how much we care about the person and his or her welfare. As we do that, our facial expression, our tone, and our posture will match our concern—and the words that come to us will be spontaneous and genuine because they will be derived from our intent. Sometimes words are actually inappropriate. If all we do is make noises of understanding, the other person will read our true feelings in our bearing. Our silent communication might thus actually be both therapeutic and eloquent.

## ∼ Ways of Listening ∼

When we engage in serious listening we find ourselves confronted by a profusion of preconceptions, biases, distractions, agendas, frustrations, suspicions, reservations, and uncertainties (both ours and the other parties'). A variety of approaches to listening have been suggested by experts to help us deal with this maze of barriers to effective understanding of one another.

## Active Listening

Active listening is promoted in much of the listening literature; it consists of committing ourselves to consciously shutting out our own thinking and then attending carefully to what the other person most wants us to hear. If we attempt active listening with sincerity, it's not difficult to do it well. Most people are so pleased to be listened to and to find that their listener is paying attention to them and even asking for more that the experience will be as wind in their sails and their verbal inhibitions will be moderated and maybe even disappear. A good active listener can actually begin to feel manipulative as the counterpart opens layer after layer of inner attitudes and feelings.

Robert Bordone writes that active listening calls upon the listener to deploy three related skills: paraphrasing, inquiry, and acknowledgment.[6]

The idea behind *paraphrasing* is to satisfy both our counterpart and us that we get the picture, accurately and fully. We need not express agreement or disagreement, and we must not try to spin our paraphrasing so that it fits our point of view. If we're even tempted to do this, we're not listening effectively, not seeking to understand; instead we're more interested in getting our point across or telling our story. It takes discipline and practice to paraphrase effectively.

*Inquiry* consists of asking questions to get at the heart of the speaker's thinking or attitude. Just as in paraphrasing, Bordone advises care to "avoid framing your inquiries as arguments," which only encourages defensiveness.

Through *acknowledgment* we convince our speaker that we not only recognize but also accept the feelings being expressed about the matter at hand; we do not attempt to deny the legitimacy of the person's perspective. It can be very difficult to avoid pointing out errors in thinking, but as soon as we go there, we are of course no longer listening. The urge to share our opinion about the matter must be suppressed—even when it's asked for—if doing so would negate the legitimacy of the person's perceptions.

If active listening feels unnatural and contrived, it's usually because we're faking it; we don't genuinely care about the other person. If we really care, we won't ever have to worry about remembering and employing a technique; our words, or even lack of words, will be the result of our genuine interest in the speaker, who will see it and believe it. We won't feel any need to argue; it would actually feel inappropriate if we did.

## Passive Listening

C. K. Gunsalus uses the term *passive listening* not as a counterpart to active listening or to suggest indifference but rather to encourage receptivity—taking it all in, soaking it up without countering.[7] She says to "spend the first two minutes listening carefully (without taking notes), not responding substantively to anything said but instead making only 'passive listening' responses intended to draw the person out: 'Really?' 'How so?' 'Tell me more about it.'" The chair can then interrupt, but only to reflect what he or she has been hearing to make sure it has been understood. Gunsalus says that a chair can also help faculty members begin solving their own problems by asking what, why, and how questions:

"What are your concerns? What, exactly, is the problem?"
"Why do you want that? Why will that solve the problem?"

"How does this address your interests? How does it affect others?"

Gunsalus encourages us to abandon our own assumptions and to "strive for a real curiosity about the other person's perspective."

## Empathic Listening

Stephen Covey promotes empathic listening as the most effective form.[8] He says that when you listen with empathy, you get "inside another person's frame of reference. You look out through it, you see the world the way they see the world, you understand their paradigm, and you understand how they feel.... The essence of empathic listening is not that you agree with someone; it's that you fully, deeply, understand that person, emotionally as well as intellectually," and that when we "listen with empathy to another person, [we] give that person psychological air. And after that vital need is met, [we] can then focus on influencing or problem solving." An important point is that the empathic listener must be prepared to be influenced by what the speaker says, to be ready to adopt a different way of viewing the world.

Covey notes that true professionals will diagnose before they prescribe and cites the example of the optometrist who recommends our glasses only after he carefully diagnoses our vision. That kind of analysis takes time. Truly effective listening also takes time, but as Covey notes, it doesn't take anywhere near as much time as it takes to back up and correct misunderstandings when you're already miles down the road.

## Deep Listening

Jim Kouzes and Barry Posner advise leaders to listen deeply enough that they can "sense the purpose in others" and discover what they desperately hope for.[9] Interestingly, they suggest that rather than taking a psychoanalytical approach with the faculty member lying on a couch, a department chair can get deep into a faculty member's life simply by taking regular breaks from routine duties, getting out of the office, and interacting with colleagues over coffee, dropping by their offices, sharing lunch, or spending some other unstructured time getting to know them and what's happening in their lives.

Recently, a young woman from our campus magazine came to my office to interview me about one of my paintings that hangs in the university library. She asked a number of questions—how I got started in oils, what it was like to move from start to finish, what my biggest challenge was, what painting meant to me, and so on. As she listened, I felt myself becoming emotional. I had been painting for fifty years, and no one had ever asked me the kinds of things this student—a stranger—was asking. Even though she was merely fulfilling an assignment, I felt that she actually cared about me and was interested in my deeper personal self. It was welcoming and validating. From that interview I learned that when we listen to get the story behind what a person does, doors open.

## Power Listening

Most of us have learned that talking is linked with power, as in winning a debate, running for a political office, teaching a course, or giving a professional seminar, and once we've been selected to serve as chair, it may feel like we're expected to speak more. However, many veteran chairs have learned that it's more powerful to listen than to talk. Consider the wise old department chair sitting back listening and processing the depths of a conversation or a group's interaction—reading faces, monitoring politics, and so on, growing ever more knowledgeable and thus also more powerful than those who can only think about what they want to say next. And when this chair does speak, it may be that it will only be to ask questions so that he or she can listen yet some more and speak only to confirm what colleagues say and why they feel the way they do. By listening this way, the chair will actually be gaining control over the situation, as well as the outcome. The chair will know where the misunderstandings are and how to resolve them.

## Self-Listening

Ron Heifetz says that when chairs are listening to all that is going on in the department or university, they can expect to "get swept up in the music" and be virtually carried away in the cacophony of other people's issues, problems, and complaints.[10] He says that the emotions associated with leadership can overpower and even derail a person. He recommends that chairs should occasionally find a sanctuary where they can "distinguish [their] inner voice from the voices that clamor for attention outside. Partners can help greatly, as can a run, a quiet walk, or a prayer to break the spell cast by the frenzy on the floor." In their sanctuary, chairs can revisit what is most important to them personally, as well as the purpose of the department and the institution, its mission, and other considerations. A little self-listening can also help chairs identify how they are doing at evaluating themselves and their perceptions. Self-listening does not suggest self-absorption; it requires that chairs keep one eye on problem faculty members and their issues and needs and the other eye on the values of the institution. Chairs who are too soft-hearted may need to remind themselves, as they sit and listen to tearful colleagues, not to forget the interests of the rest of the faculty who are not crying.

### ∿ Listening Tips for Chairs ∿

In addition to considering the various ways of listening that others have suggested, here are a few additional tips for chairs who wish to take listening seriously.

- **Be Mindful of Bias.** We all have filters located somewhere between our ears and our brains. These are cultural and experiential and are shaped by our preconceptions and preferences such that the things that we want to hear slip through more easily than the things we've become accustomed to ignoring or blocking out. Chairs should constantly accuse themselves and their colleagues who agree with them of being biased and ask what their biases might be. This is very difficult to do. Simply attempting to become better informed doesn't help and may actually fortify our biases. As I write this, we are in the midst of bitter partisan conflicts in America. It is discouraging to notice how I tend to entertain only the ideas, opinions, and expressions that support what I have felt for years, and my brain (I can feel it) tends to resist any efforts I make to be open to the other side's perspective.

- **Be Mindful of Gender.** Men and women speak and listen differently. Deborah Tannen writes that girls are prone to "growing up invisible" as they observe that the men in their families tell stories and the women listen.[11] She notes that boys learn that "giving information ... frames one in a position of higher status, while the act of listening frames one as lower." She tells us that "when women listen to men, they are not thinking in terms of status."

Another important gender difference is that when talking about concerns or difficulties, each gender anticipates a different kind of response. Women tend to focus on interpersonal relationships and are skilled at the indirect approach, whereas men focus on being direct and address practical issues or solutions. When women take the more masculine approach, they can be viewed less favorably and even as less competent by both men and women.

We can thus appreciate that a woman chair interacting with a challenging male member of the faculty faces a much different package of issues and the associated potential for misunderstanding than when interacting with another woman— and of course the same is true for the male chair interacting with a woman or another man. The important thing to remember is that neither gender is wrong, foolish, or clueless; the two are simply different. If we're sensitive to this, we'll at least be open to the need to tread carefully and consider the listening presumptions associated with our gender.

• **Welcome Complaints and Criticism**. Research has shown that particularly when confronted with criticism, leaders perceive themselves as better listeners than they actually are.[12] The same is undoubtedly true when we're asked to listen to complaints. One survey respondent wrote, "I learned that as cranky as some of my colleagues can be, there is always a seed of truth in their complaints. Therefore, I listen very carefully when my colleagues speak."

Notice that a complaint is usually a statement of value. There is some condition or practice that the complainer wishes would replace whatever it is that seems exasperating. Bashing or whining is seldom constructive, but a complaint can nevertheless be useful. So upon fielding a protest, consider saying something like "Let's leverage your concern. What is it that you value? What would you like to see happen instead? What do you recommend? What can you do?"

After we've listened, maybe longer than we ever wanted, it's often helpful to ask for yet more. We can say things like "Can you take that further for me? I sense that there's more to it, and I don't think I understand it." When we keep asking for more and others open up, they often begin to find an answer to their own problems. In fact, asking a question of colleagues relieves us of the burden of attempting to tell them what to do. "What do you think should be done?" or "What do you recommend?" not only lobs the problem back into their court but also reduces the possibility of their becoming dependent on us to solve their problems.

---

> "Listen, but ban whining."
>
> —*Survey comment*

---

## ∿ A Final Thought on Listening ∿

Before we leave Step 5, let's return to Anna and Walter. We left them in Chapter One with Walter having abstained from supporting the department's measures-of-excellence document. Was there a listening opportunity for Anna at that point? Might she have gone to Walter's office and said something like "Hi, Walter. I've come to see if you can help me. As you can tell, I feel that our measures-of-excellence guidelines are important to the department; we've worked on them for almost a year, and now that they've been voted up, we'll be following them. As I move to overseeing their implementation, your thoughts could be helpful to me. Would you be willing to talk about your abstention? Let me listen."

Sound a little risky? How could Anna minimize the tension? Let's try moving back even further—back to the time when Anna and her colleagues first went public with their measures-of-excellence project. Anna would have known then that Walter, who was no fool, would probably have viewed the project as a response to his behavior and perhaps even have felt that the whole effort was aimed at him personally. Being aware of this and anticipating Walter's reaction when and if their document ever came up for a vote, Anna might have started laying some listening groundwork with Walter by going out of her way to notice and recognize him, to call on him for guidance based on a genuine department need, and to share something with him around a common interest that she could have identified through casual interaction (see "deep listening" earlier in this chapter). If Anna had done these things over the nine months between his outburst in the faculty meeting and the department vote on the guidelines, we might expect that the tension would be diminished, that Anna's body language would draw on the relationship she had built with Walter (which body language he would be reading with considerable accuracy), and that he might actually share with her how he was feeling.

If Anna had not prepared that listening ground and had not let Walter know that she recognized and appreciated his talents and valued his membership in the department, the tension as she spoke with Walter about his abstention would naturally be high. Walter might not explode at her, although he had a reputation for doing just that, but he might become passive-aggressive or perhaps isolate himself in his office, feeling excluded (comparable to suffering) in a state of productivity decline.

As you can see, effective listening takes planning and preparation; we don't just walk in on someone and say, "I'm here to listen." It also takes patience and practice. Perhaps nowhere else in the six steps do we find a better fit for "there's no quick fix." Just as playing the piano requires practice, so does listening. Feeling impatient with ourselves and especially with the other person is normal. Yet unlike the slowness of the piano to respond to our fingers, our counterparts sometimes respond so quickly to our overtures to understand them that their eagerness can surprise and even startle us.

## Summary for Step 5: Listen

- Warm up to your colleagues and get to know them before you attempt to listen to them.

- Effective listening means wanting very much to understand the other person's story.

- Be ever mindful of your own biases and prejudices.

- When it's time to listen, avoid the overpowering temptation to talk.

- Listen with your eyes and your heart.

- Study and practice effective listening skills.

## Notes

1. A. F. Lucas. (1994). *Strengthening departmental leadership: A team-building guide for chairs in colleges and universities* (pp. 89–93). San Francisco: Jossey-Bass.

2. D. Rock. (2009). Managing with the brain in mind. *Oxford Leadership Journal, 1*(1), 1. Retrieved from http://www.oxfordleadership.com/journal/vol1_issue1/rock.pdf

3. T. Fiutak, personal communication, January 18, 1992.

4. D. R. Leaming. (2007). *Academic leadership: A practical guide to chairing the department* (2nd ed., pp. 347–348). Bolton, MA: Anker.

5. K. Patterson, J. Grenny, D. Maxfield, R. McMillan, & A. Switzler. (2008). *Influencer: The power to change anything* (pp. 50–51). New York: McGraw-Hill.

6. R. C. Bordone. (2007). Listen up! Your talks may depend on it. *Negotiation Newsletter, 10*(5), 9–11.

7. C. K. Gunsalus. (2006). *The college administrator's survival guide* (pp. 73–76). Cambridge, MA: Harvard University Press.

8. S. R. Covey. (1989). *The seven habits of highly effective people: Restoring the character ethic* (pp. 239–253). New York: Simon & Schuster.

9. J. M. Kouzes & B. Z. Posner. (2003). *Academic administrator's guide to exemplary leadership* (pp. 43–44). San Francisco: Jossey-Bass.

10. R. A. Heifetz. (1994). *Leadership without easy answers* (p. 273). Cambridge, MA: Harvard University Press.

11. D. Tannen. (1990). *You just don't understand: Women and men in conversation* (pp. 136–139). New York: Morrow.

12. P. Barwise & S. Meehan. (2008). So you think you're a good listener. *Harvard Business Review, 86*(4), 22.

# CHAPTER SIX

# Step 6: Take Effective Action

## Anna Revisited

*In Chapter One we left Anna and Walter just as their department had adopted a measures-of-excellence document with a near-unanimous vote. Walter had been one of two members who abstained.*

*In the department's first faculty meeting following adoption of the document, an assistant professor was presenting a proposal on redesigning the General Education service course when Walter interrupted with "Good grief, Justin, do you think you're working at a prep school? We're a highly-regarded institution, and we have a time-honored tradition of first-class offerings from this department. We serve the entire campus. This is a crappy idea, and you're doing a crappy job of presenting it. I'm not so much disappointed as I am disgusted. Did somebody help you with this, or did you screw it up all by yourself?"*

> *Walter then moved his outstretched arms around the room as if beseeching his colleagues to join him in his assessment or perhaps to say, "I lay my case before you; someone take it from here."*

I have titled this chapter "Take Effective Action." By this I mean not just taking steps to reduce or arrest problem behavior but also responding in a way that is appropriate for the given situation and that is compliant with institutional procedures.

What action would be effective for Anna to take? Walter was apparently testing whether his abstention from voting on the performance expectations document exempted him from compliance, or maybe he was demonstrating that he had not made any promise to conform to what he felt the others had sucked up to. Unless Anna had anticipated something like this, unless she had considered what she would do if Walter acted up again, chances are Anna really wouldn't know what to do.

## ∿ Be Prepared ∿

It's a high-stakes moment. How Anna responds will have a huge impact on the future health and morale of the department and on her status in the eyes of her colleagues. This was no time to default to the department's history of remaining silent and looking at the floor, which had given Walter license to misbehave for years. Either the faculty will see their months of work in preparing their behavioral code upheld, or they will be disappointed in their leader for wimping out. At the same time, the faculty will want Anna to respond appropriately to

Walter. She must not let the lizard in her rise up and commandeer her brain to the point that she joins Walter in violating the behavioral code herself.

The Boy Scouts' motto "Be Prepared" comes to mind. What could Anna have done to be prepared for Walter's outburst? The first five steps covered in the preceding chapters each concluded with a list of effective actions for dealing with problem faculty. Let's revisit them to see how they could have helped Anna prepare for what Walter had just done:

- **Step 1: Clarify Values and Expectations.** Anna and her colleagues had done a nice job of implementing Step 1; they had clarified their department's values and expectations. Walter was putting their standard to the test, but Anna and her colleagues had the advantage of having a clear and collective sense of what was important to them in how their department worked together; it was now their opportunity to uphold their standards.
- **Step 2: Follow Policy.** We don't know how well prepared Anna was here. Had she visited with the director of faculty relations to discuss what her options were in case Walter was belligerent in public (or in private) again? Was there a policy for dealing with incivility or bullying? How would the people in the legal office advise her? What was she *not* to do? Think how much more confident Anna would have been in that meeting if she had been appropriately informed.
- **Step 3: Build Trust with Colleagues.** It had been almost a year since Walter's behavior triggered the development of the department's behavioral code. During that time, what had Anna done to build trust with key colleagues? Had she demonstrated and encouraged the kind of behavior addressed in the department's code? Had she visited with senior respected members of the faculty to ensure that they were committed

and prepared to help her defend their collective expectations? Had Anna warmed up to Walter over the previous months? Consider the strength of Anna's position at the moment of Walter's second outburst if she had been able to answer yes to these questions.

> "The number one critical success factor for me has been to maintain a close relationship with two groups: one or two senior faculty members with long institutional memory (respected by the department) and other department chairs with more experience than me."
>
> —*Survey comment*

• **Step 4: Evaluate Yourself and Your Perceptions.** Here are some self-evaluation questions for Anna. While the department's behavioral code was being developed, had she reevaluated not only how she spoke about Walter but also how she thought about him? Had she considered what changes she might have made in her own behavior to be better able to work with him? Had she pondered what might be the cause of Walter's challenging behavior? Had she been quick to observe (notice and obey) what she felt she should do?

• **Step 5: Listen.** At the end of Chapter Five we reviewed what Anna might have done to earn the right to approach Walter and listen to him. This included stopping by his office to engage in small talk and to affirm the value of his many contributions, asking for his opinion and even inviting him to share his thinking at the next faculty meeting. If Anna had earned the right to ask Walter to talk with her and honed her listening skills, it is possible that Walter would have revealed some inner struggle or personal problem and thus have vented his feelings more privately and constructively.

How much time had Anna spent chatting with friends about Walter compared to studying and working on skills that would have helped her either rehabilitate or discipline him? Anna's ability to respond appropriately and effectively to Walter's outburst would be in direct relation to the amount of time and energy she put into researching and thinking about the best response and deliberately "practicing" the skills needed, much like the Olympic hopefuls mentioned in Step 4.

## ∿ Act Quickly ∿

When confronted with problem behavior, it's important to deal with it as promptly as possible. Walter's behavior demands an immediate and uncompromising response. Even if he had been less abusive in his remark to Justin but still managed to be insulting, Anna would have been derelict to let it pass without instantly responding with something like "Walter, that comment violates the civility agreement we have in this department. Would you please express your concern in a manner that will meet with our approval?"

> "Never allow persistent misbehavior by any faculty member."
> —*Survey comment*

A chair should never wink at or ignore substandard conduct, no matter who has done it. If a faculty member is performing poorly, engaging in conflict-of-interest activities, passive-aggressively resisting conformity, or any other problematic behavior, the chair should intervene quickly. Overlooking or discounting any deviant behavior establishes a culture of tolerance and mediocrity that invariably leads to decay.

With Anna's department having just produced and accepted a new standard, it was critical that she respond immediately to Walter's defiance.

Given Walter's behavior, Anna should conclude the meeting with something like "Folks, this meeting is adjourned. Walter, come with me to my office. Bruce, will you join us please?" She should say this with as much composure as she can muster, and to protect herself, she should say no more. This would send a signal to everyone that the new behavioral code was being upheld—better to show it than to say it. Bruce is the most respected colleague in the department. He has been invited for two reasons. First, it makes it easier for Walter to comply with Anna's request, and second, Bruce will serve as a witness. Anna would clarify Bruce's witness status as soon as the door to her office was closed, letting both Bruce and Walter know that Bruce was there to safeguard both Walter's interests and her own.

## ∿ Have a Witness and Keep Notes ∿

It is always wise to secure a witness whenever meeting with someone who may become emotional or volatile or when you are delivering information that could be upsetting, even if the recipient is normally calm. Having the right third party in the room can be reassuring and supportive, for the chair and also for the faculty member. Someone from human resources may be a good choice. It is my experience that if you are alone in a room with someone and find yourself wishing there was a third person present, you should stand up and open the door. Explain that the discussion has become sensitive and that to be fair to everyone and to be sure that you are following policy, you are going to postpone the conversation until a third person can join you.

From a legal standpoint, a witness can be most helpful in providing verification of what was said. If possible, both of you should take notes. However, Don Chu wisely suggests discretion when taking notes. "What is your campus human resources policy on taking personal notes of meetings?" he asks. "Evidence of who said what to whom and when may be important in a personnel case. But remember that notes may be subpoenaed."[1]

If it is inconvenient or impolite to take notes during the visit, a summary should be written as soon as possible after the meeting and never delayed until even the next day. It can be helpful to share your notes with the other party, perhaps in an e-mail. This can be accompanied by a request that the person let you know if you captured things correctly or forgot something. The summary and response serve as a record of the meeting and can be helpful later, especially if any sort of agreement was made and later challenged.

A word of caution: chairs should bear in mind that all of their notes and records, including e-mails to colleagues, are subject to discovery for legal purposes. It's wise to remain as objective as possible in both your interactions and your notes. Avoid accusatory or judgmental statements by using language such as "seeming disregard" of the rules or "apparent offense." In any situation that deals with policy or where emotions may be a factor, it is wise to share a draft of your notes or e-mail with someone from human resources and the dean before sending them to the faculty member.

As Chu points out, in all your interactions with the faculty member, it is important to ensure that their rights are protected:

> While attempting to deal with problematic faculty or staff, make sure that their rights are also represented. Due process is a legal term with campus-specific definitions

usually found in faculty bylaws or in human resources policy documents.[2]

Due process refers to the right that people have to be informed of any decisions or actions taken against them, including the right to appeal and to engage the assistance of a neutral party.

## ∿ Confront with Confidence ∿

The authors of *Crucial Confrontations* point out that "confrontations comprise the very foundation of accountability. They all start with the question: 'Why didn't you do what you were supposed to do?' . . . Confrontations are the prickly, complicated, and often frightening performance discussions that keep you up nights."[3] Interestingly, before confronting anyone, they recommend beginning with Step 4, "evaluate yourself and your perceptions."

> When we approach a crucial confrontation it's important to know that we must work on ourselves first. . . . Here's how those who master crucial confrontations make sure their thoughts are in order before they put their mouths in gear: . . . They make sure that the thoughts rushing around in their heads—their facts, stories, and emotions—help them to see the other person as a person rather than a villain.[4]

In his chapter titled "Dealing with Difficult Faculty," Deryl Leaming makes a wise recommendation:

> Allow others the opportunity to save face. It is human nature to want to crush those who attack us, but

everyone is better served if difficult faculty members are given a way to save face. This is one of the reasons to avoid public reprimands of faculty or staff. Permitting a person to save face is a gracious gesture, though one occasionally gets comments like "You had your chance to get even; why didn't you?" or something similar. Good leadership is not about getting even.[5]

I look back regretfully on an occasion when I didn't follow Leaming's counsel. I was a dean. A group of about thirty faculty members from our college were gathered to consider the progress we were making on an initiative that had caused considerable angst across the college; more than a few noses had been bent. My associate dean was leading the meeting. Almost as soon as he started speaking, two members of the faculty stood, one after the other, and accused him of "lying again." I stood up and asked the two accusers to either apologize or leave the room so that we could proceed with civility. I then scolded both of them. They left, as did another member of the faculty who had said nothing. I stayed in the room with everyone else; tension was high.

When the meeting was over, I found an e-mail from the silent faculty member who had left the room; it read: "I applaud your principled stand; but you went too far. You set yourself up as better than them and lectured. I left the room not as an expression of support of their behavior but as an expression of lack of support for yours." Although several members of the faculty, including my associate dean, thanked me for "standing up to those guys," I have always felt that the content of that e-mail was a very insightful appraisal of my behavior; I should have simply invited the two to restate their concerns without reprimanding them.

So if Anna has appropriately withdrawn to her office, which is a safe private setting, and if she has Bruce as a witness, what should she say? I like the advice of Ron McMillan, who says that a confrontation should start by "describing the gap [between] what happened compared with what was expected. Next, ask why it happened this way."[6] Note that doing this requires that expectations have been made clear and are understood so that the gap between those expectations and the person's conduct is obvious. Anna is on solid footing here. She might say, "Walter, what you just said to Justin was inappropriate. It was a personal attack and violated our department's code. Talk to me about the gap between our expectations and what you did."

## ∽ Clarify and Impose Consequences ∽

If Anna confronts Walter by asking him to talk to her about the gap, we might expect him to attempt to justify his behavior or to brush it off. Anna would then have the opportunity to discuss consequences. She would need to make sure that Walter understood that complying with the department's code was not just a suggestion; it was a *requirement* of his job. In other words, she would need to help Walter understand that in addition to the various natural consequences of his behavior (Justin's feeling abused, the faculty's being upset, and Walter's slipping in esteem), there would be the consequences that she and the administration would impose on him if he didn't comply with what was required of everyone. She might say something like "Walter, we greatly value your skills and contributions, but we have to consider the accompanying cost of your conduct, the negative impact on our department climate."

If Walter continued in belligerence, either in her office or later, it would be essential for Anna to clarify that his failure to comply with expectations was resulting in disciplinary steps being taken (for which she should seek guid-

*It is more important to do what is best for the team rather than continue to struggle at rescuing a habitually disruptive comrade.*

ance from human resources and approval from the dean). This would represent a very serious step and would probably erode any relationship that remained between Anna and Walter. But whenever a person's conduct damages the productivity and quality of life of the entire unit, it is more important to do what is best for the team rather than continue to struggle at rescuing a habitually disruptive comrade.

Having to deal with someone like Walter is not a common occurrence. More typically, chairs find themselves considering how to work with a faculty member who is polite but whose performance has slipped in some minor way. What if it had been someone else in Anna's office—a younger collegial person whose teaching was substandard (subpar student ratings, significant student complaints, or frequent late arrival to class) toward whom Anna felt protective? We can all understand that in such a case, Anna's sense of compassion might lead her to attempt to shield her younger colleague from imposed consequences. But enabling anyone, regardless of age or status, to misbehave or operate below standards, especially repeatedly, weakens both them and the department. Clarifying the gap between expectations and people's performance and asking them to talk about it with you is a respectful means of helping them see and understand how they are perceived and gives them the opportunity to recommend corrective action.

## An Expectations-and-Consequences Formula

My colleague David Whetten has spent thirty-five years at two universities researching factors that influence behavior and performance. He has developed a performance formula:

$$\text{Performance} = \text{expectations} \times \text{ability} \times \text{motivation}$$

If people know what is expected of them, their performance then depends on whether they can and will meet expectations. Note that the components of Whetten's formula are multiplicative; if any one of the elements is zero, performance is zero. High expectations combined with high motivation won't lead to measurable productivity if ability is absent. How a chair handles all three aspects—expectations, ability, and motivation—is critical.

### Expectations

"If you find yourself frustrated with or disappointed in someone," writes C. K. Gunsalus, "it may be worth considering whether you've ever let him or her know, in a positive way, what you expect."[7]

Having an expectations document for the department is a good start, but a chair needs to meet individually with any faculty members who are not meeting expectations and explore whether they understand what is specifically expected of them, what acceptable performance looks like in their case, and whether they feel there is any reason the standards might not apply to them. "Expectations are the deal breaker," Whetten says. "If there is uncertainty around expectations people will undergo performance stress of the worst kind."[8]

### Ability

The next step is to determine whether a "problem" faculty member has the appropriate skills and resources to do what is expected. "Do you have what you need to meet expectations?"

the chair can ask. Perhaps there's a need to update skills through a professional leave, a workshop, or a sabbatical. Could supplemental resources (from the department or the dean) be helpful?

A common error is for the chair to confuse ability with motivation. If someone isn't measuring up, it's easy to conclude that the person doesn't care or is just lazy. The condition of illiteracy is not a problem we often encounter in academe, but it illustrates how a lack of ability may appear to be a lack of motivation. A person who can't read will go to extreme measures to hide that deficiency and may even become insubordinate or claim lack of motivation rather than disclose the embarrassing handicap. With today's speed of advances in knowledge and technology, it is not uncommon for senior faculty members in some fields to find themselves hopelessly behind and hesitant or even afraid to disclose their deficiency. With appropriate sensitivity, a chair can usually find a way to determine whether a faculty member has the requisite skill or ability to meet expectations.

### *Motivation*

Chairs must be cautious when attempting to evaluate a faculty member's motivation. Most leaders are prone to focus on motivation without first clarifying expectations and assessing ability. Only after expectations and ability have been considered and all misunderstandings removed should the chair even think of asking, "Is your heart really in this?"

Although it's not the chair's job to motivate a faculty member, the chair's actions can affect motivation considerably, notably by how consequences are managed. Patterson and colleagues point out:

> *Consequences motivate.* Motivation isn't something you do to someone. People already want to do things. They're motivated by the consequences they anticipate. And since

any action leads to a variety of consequences, people act on the basis of the overall consequence bundle.[9]

Given this insight, Whetten's formula could be rewritten as

Performance = expectations $\times$ ability $\times$ *consequences*

Whetten specifies that a chair must be consistent in the application of consequences and that not responding can create problems. If performance is poor and nothing is done, the faculty member will likely assume that no one really cares, and the poor behavior can be expected to continue or perhaps become worse. On the other hand, if performance is favorable and nothing is done, the faculty member may assume that no one is paying attention and abandon the extra effort.

It's important to note that effective consequences do not consist of just talking; they are based on something happening: a privilege lost or a reward provided. Giving or withholding a salary increase or the opportunity to teach summer classes are common tactics, as are considerations of travel approval. Rewards might consist of recommendations for recognitions and awards, approval to serve on key committees, or something as simple as a congratulatory note. Also, for expectations and consequences to be effective, they must be large enough to make a difference to the faculty member who otherwise might be willing to lose a small perk or two in order to continue to operate somewhere below the standard.

> "For problem faculty, establish behavior goals that require immediate and sustained change. Warn faculty they may lose some privileges (e.g., summer teaching) if change does not occur."
>
> —*Survey comment*

Gunsalus has a surprising recommendation when it comes to handling consequences. She suggests that chairs read a book on dog training, pointing out that just as with dogs, consistency with people is essential: one should *always* reward good behavior and should *never* reward bad behavior.[10] She shared with me that when visiting universities, she often encounters situations where an administrator is thinking of providing a reward such as a significant pay increase for a problem faculty member in the hope that it will motivate the person to come around.

Even after she has discussed the necessity of always rewarding good behavior and never rewarding bad, Gunsalus frequently has administrators say to her, "You're right in principle, of course, but surely you'll agree that in my case, an exception is warranted." This line of thinking was verified in one of the responses to the survey: "For those that are not interested in being part of the group—give them everything they want so they don't complain or get in the way of progress."

To such thinking Gunsalus always replies, "What part of *never* don't you understand?"[11]

## ∿ Assemble a Solid Case (Document, Document, Document) ∿

One of the most common frustrations I hear expressed by administrators is failure on their part, or on the part of the chair or chairs that preceded them, to adequately document problem behavior that has persisted for some time. Chairs should take notes and keep records of all annual reviews, performance appraisals, tenure and promotion difficulties, complaints (including students'), e-mail correspondence, and anything else that might one day come under scrutiny or necessitate disciplinary action. This means that an outside party viewing the file would be able to determine whether the interests of both the university and the faculty member were properly considered and addressed. If expectations are clarified, in writing, and notes are kept as to whether they were met, most participants are prepared to accept appropriate consequences. It's the track record that counts. Surprises are never appropriate and often won't be sustained if challenged in court. Too often the action that is regarded as the "last straw" after years of bad behavior actually ends up being the first time anyone considered documenting it.

As mentioned before, it is important to act on things quickly; the longer a problem goes unchecked, the more difficult it can be to correct. If chairs and administrators have stood silently by for months or years, their silence or inaction is often interpreted to mean that the unchallenged behavior has their blessing. There's an old English word, *estoppel*, that is still used in today's courts. An example of its application would be in the situation where a patent holder waits several years to sue someone who has infringed on his patent. He may be estopped by the courts from proceeding with an infringement suit because his long delay led the infringer to assume that the patent was never going to be enforced. There are numerous examples of how a long period of permissiveness not only makes it difficult ultimately to take corrective action but can be legally interpreted as approval.

On the matter of building a solid case, there is at least one university where helpful and corrective action is formalized into policy based on three progressive steps that, contrary to the resigned conclusion of the survey comment on the following page, prove to be both considerate and effective.

1. When a chair prepares for the annual review of a faculty member whose performance over the previous year has not met expectations, an assessment is made to determine whether

"I have a great team except for one person who used to be a despotic chair. With her I have tried many different approaches (giving her new responsibilities, recognizing her experience, asking for her advice), but everything has failed. I think that in most departments there are people too damaged from past circumstances that it is impossible to change them. Universities cannot do anything to help. That's my experience. I have been patient, that is it."

—*Survey comment*

it is an anomaly. Anyone can have a bad year. It is important, however, in the context of goodwill and encouragement, for the chair to note—in discussion with the poor performer and in follow-up correspondence—that acceptable performance is anticipated and expected the following year. The conversation and correspondence should clearly specify what acceptable performance will look like. The chair should thoughtfully explore ways that he or she and the department might help. Consequences for failing to meet expectations should also be made clear and, depending on the severity of the situation, might include the possibility of termination should egregious behavior continue. Appropriate documentation is critical.

2. If, one year after the errant behavior was noted and discussed, the poor performance or misconduct has not been rectified, the chair is expected to advance the case and involve the dean. The dean and chair together consider the circumstances and visit with the faculty member to determine what can be done. Perhaps the dean has access to resources that will help turn the situation around (note the temptation to reward bad behavior; this is not what calling on the dean's resources should

entail). Of course, the dean's involvement adds a level of seriousness to the situation, and the onus for improvement is increased. Consequences for failing to meet expectations are again made clear; documentation at this point may include an official letter of reprimand or warning (which could also have been issued back at step 1 if the issue were major). Involving the dean in a case is considered to constitute two strikes out of three. Human resources and perhaps legal counsel will likely be apprised and consulted.

3.  A situation that continues to be problematic into a third year and thus lands in the lap of the assistant provost is rare. The intent of progressive levels of administrative involvement is constructive—to assist the faculty member who is struggling and to provide a pathway to a successful outcome. The purpose is not to accumulate an overwhelming case against a misfortunate who has fallen on bad luck. However, if the person has not been responsive to encouragement and support, a strong case for dismissal will be the result.

Careful documentation and periodic interaction (between chair and faculty member and between chair and dean or faculty relations director or both) during each year of these progressive steps is assumed. Note that this three-step process is most effective for cases where remediation appears probable. Dismissal of a person for egregious violation of the rules, the honor code, the law, or other serious infractions need not be delayed. Also, circumstances may dictate that the steps be ratcheted up and occur over a period of months rather than years.

## ∿ Be Patient ∿

When someone has just added the last straw and you're the camel, the advice to be patient might not go down very well.

Yet patience is something a chair needs to strive for while standing up to the offender. First, if the chair and his or her predecessors have only grumbled to themselves and to each other about a colleague's behavior for years, that colleague deserves to be granted some time to adjust to the new modus operandi. This doesn't mean that the chair needs to tolerate misconduct any longer, but it does mean that the offender can't be expected to become disentangled from a habit that has been reinforced for years and reform overnight.

Second, the chair would be wise to own up to the fact that the trouble the faculty and the department are in is not just about the problem colleague; it's about all of them. The chair might even address this point when talking with the problematic colleague by saying, "Let me include an apology here. This department has been deceitful with you. We've been upset by your behavior for years, and we've never let you know how we feel. We've failed you. It has taken us too long to deal honestly with you." By not casting the colleague as a lone villain, the chair would be helping the person save face, which should reduce defensiveness. In any event, the chair would be wise to strive for patience while initiating what is a totally new world for the colleague and for the department.

## ∿ Weigh the Costs ∿

Deryl Leaming asks, "Is a faculty member's 'problem' exacting any cost or value, or is it something that simply annoys you?"[12] He then cites Clayton Sherman, who writes, "If an actual calculation of costs shows that the situation is no big deal, then relax. Neither the world nor the people in it are perfect, and maybe the answer is just to accept life's realities with good grace."[13]

Daniel Levin offers the following advice:

Be thankful for anyone in your life who's a problem. They're your teachers, for they show you where you truly stand. A great saint once said to a disciple who came to him complaining about someone else: "He is your greatest blessing. In fact, if he were not here, it would behoove us to go out and find one like him."[14]

Bob Sutton asks us to resist the temptation to apply a derogatory label to everyone "who annoys you or has a bad moment. . . . Some people with the roughest exteriors have the biggest hearts once you get to know them—I call them porcupines with hearts of gold."[15]

## Summary for Step 6: Take Effective Action

- Prepare in advance for (anticipate) problem interactions; follow all the steps.

- Act quickly; never wink at or ignore violations of expectations or protocol.

- Confront offenders in private; describe the gap between expectations and conduct.

- Have a witness to contentious discussions, and keep notes that are fair and accurate.

- Assemble a solid case; it's the track record or pattern that counts.

- Impose consequences; always reward good behavior; never reward bad.

- Be patient; accept some of the blame, and remember that porcupines often have hearts of gold.

# Notes

1. D. Chu. (2006). *The department chair primer: Leading and managing academic departments* (pp. 77, 78). Bolton, MA: Anker.

2. D. Chu. (2006). *The department chair primer: Leading and managing academic departments* (p. 80). Bolton, MA: Anker.

3. K. Patterson, J. Grenny, R. McMillan, & A. Switzler. (2005). *Crucial confrontations: Tools for resolving broken promises, violated expectations, and bad behavior* (p. xvii). New York: McGraw-Hill.

4. K. Patterson, J. Grenny, R. McMillan, & A. Switzler. (2005). *Crucial confrontations: Tools for resolving broken promises, violated expectations, and bad behavior* (p. 23). New York: McGraw-Hill.

5. D. R. Leaming. (2007). *Academic leadership: A practical guide to chairing the department* (2nd ed.; p. 348). Bolton, MA: Anker.

6. R. McMillan. (2009, October 14). Working with a difficult employee. *Crucial Skills Newsletter, 7*(41). Retrieved from http://www.vitalsmarts.com/

7. C. K. Gunsalus, (2006). *The college administrator's survival guide* (p. 18). Cambridge, MA: Harvard University Press.

8. D. Whetten, personal communication, January 9, 2012.

9. K. Patterson, J. Grenny, R. McMillan, & A. Switzler. (2005). *Crucial confrontations: Tools for resolving broken promises, violated expectations, and bad behavior* (pp. 143–144). New York: McGraw-Hill.

10. C. K. Gunsalus. (2006). *The college administrator's survival guide* (p. 71). Cambridge, MA: Harvard University Press.

11. C. K. Gunsalus, personal communication, April 9, 2008.

12. D. R. Leaming. (2007). *Academic leadership: A practical guide to chairing the department* (2nd ed.; p. 339). Bolton, MA: Anker.

13. V. C. Sherman. (1987). *From losers to winners: How to manage problem employees … and what to do if you can't* (rev. ed.; p. 83). New York: American Management Association.

14. D. Levin. (2005). *The Zen book* (p. 34). Carlsbad, CA: Hay House.

15. R. I. Sutton. (2007). *The no asshole rule: Building a civilized workplace and surviving one that isn't* (pp. 87–88). New York: Warner Business Books.

# PART TWO

# Tough Questions

The chapters in Part Two tackle five specific problem faculty characters that chairs have asked about most often. These chairs have said, "The six steps are helpful, but what about ..."

- **The Chronic Poor Performer?** The poor performer appears to be the most common type of problem faculty. Some chairs even seem to accept that poor performance constitutes part of a normal distribution of people. The fact is that poor performance, though common, should not be accepted, and it is not difficult to correct.
- **The Passive-Aggressive Colleague?** Somewhere between poor performers and bullies we find passive-aggressive colleagues. These people may overlap with poor performers or bullies and often present the most frustrating problems for both chairs and their department colleagues.
- **Bullies?** Bullies are usually viewed as the most challenging of all problem faculty, and there is good reason for this. Remediation of a bully is not an intuitive process and requires special preparation and understanding.
- **The Problem Characters Who Emerge During Times of Change?** Change usually exposes a range of character types that a chair might have never appreciated or even noticed in the faculty. These distinctive characters may prove especially problematic if their needs and expectations are not understood.
- **The Psychologically Impaired?** These faculty members appear to be more common than we realize and like many of us may fluctuate from near-normal behavior to an impaired state and back again. Most chairs feel inadequate in their interactions with these individuals.

Each of the five chapters in Part Two starts with a chair-centered decision case or dilemma. Like all the profiles in this book, the cases are real, although they have been disguised. Customized chair-helpful steps are provided throughout each chapter and summarized at the end.

# CHAPTER SEVEN

# What About the Chronic Poor Performer?

## Reese

*Reese was chair of the Accounting Department. He was meeting with Clarence for his annual performance evaluation. Clarence was a sixty-one-year-old professor who had previously been suitably productive but whose scholarship had slipped to an unacceptable level. His service to the profession and to the department had also declined. He no longer served on national committees, frequently skipped faculty meetings, and had been slow in fulfilling department assignments. Clarence's teaching scores were about average for the department. This had been the pattern for some time. Reese had been hesitant to confront Clarence, who was a very congenial colleague; they golfed together sometimes. Lately, however, Reese had realized that his failure to confront Clarence constituted tacit approval, if not actual support, of his poor performance. Their department was ranked in the top twenty-five nationally, and Reese had felt the onus of at least sustaining that ranking if not helping the department move up a little.*

*After an exchange of pleasantries, Reese shared the latest national rankings with Clarence and placed a copy of the department's performance standards on the table. After thanking Clarence for his part in helping the department become exemplary, Reese opened the performance standards to the scholarship section and asked Clarence to talk with him about the gap between the standards and his own productivity over the past three years.*

*Clarence responded with "Reese, you know my specialty. It takes years to complete a study; there's no quick route to publications. And after all I've done for this place, it owes me, don't you think?"*

Clarence's case is not atypical. Poor performers are usually those who have achieved tenure and carry on well for a number of years and then slip to an unacceptable level of productivity—in teaching, research, service, or all three. In some cases they have been plateaued at a level of low productivity for years and show few signs of caring about it. Sometimes the poor performer is a new hire; the chair must deal with such a situation promptly. Comments returned by two chairs in the national survey document experience and wisdom: "Burning up good faculty while avoiding or ignoring poor ones is a real temptation that has to be effectively resisted," said one respondent. "Never avoid or delay the hard task of requiring improvement or outlining poor performance," said another. "If not dealt with, the unkindest thing of all will eventually result."

## ∿ Start with Expectations ∿

In considering how Reese might have responded to Clarence, let's revisit Whetten's performance formula:

Performance = expectations × ability × motivation

Notice that in Clarence's case, *motivation* jumps out and invites us to conclude not only that he had become lazy but also that Reese ought to talk with him about his enthusiasm. Recall, however, what Whetten said: we should always start with *expectations*, and that until we can come to an agreement about expectations, we will make little, if any, progress with performance. With expectations in mind, let's consider Clarence's comment: "You know my specialty. It takes years to complete a study; there's no quick route to publications."

Reese might have done well to acknowledge that some departmental specialties were more conducive to the quick delivery of scholarly products than others. He could then point out that Clarence had previously managed to publish frequently, and others in his discipline were still doing it. Reese would want to stand firm in upholding the department's publication standard, working with Clarence to specify acceptable performance in measurable particulars, such as the number and type of scholarly products and by what date, and also not overlook the expected amount and quality of committee service, attendance and input at meetings, and other benchmarks. This could have easily been done in a congenial and supportive manner, with Reese asking Clarence how he as chair or the department might help.

What about Clarence's comment "After all I've done for this place, it owes me, don't you think?" Of course it would be appropriate for Reese to acknowledge Clarence's many years of service and to thank him, citing some specific examples. It would then be time to respond to Clarence's retort directly. Based on the gap between his performance and the department's expectations, could it not be concluded that Clarence actually owed the institution? He had been accepting paychecks and benefits for some time but had been performing below an acceptable level. The point Reese would want to communicate was that for the institution to continue to honor its contract, it would be necessary for Clarence to comply with the institution's expectations. It would have been unwise to proceed any further in their discussion until they both agreed on what was expected of Clarence in his position at that time.

Before we move on to considering ability and motivation, it might be helpful to stop and consider other possible poor performance scenarios not relevant to the Clarence case. There could be any number of possible reasons for a faculty member's productivity to decline, and chairs should be quick to observe their colleague's responses and body language when confronting the person about it. The faculty member might look at the floor, for example, and say something like "Yeah, I really ought to be doing better, but ..."

If the chair has established a good relationship with the person and is careful to watch body language as well as listen to words and tones, he or she might discover something in the faculty member's life that warrants special consideration, such as a wayward child, a ruined marriage, or a developing personal disability. Some issues warrant special understanding, but if they have resulted in prolonged underperformance, it will still be wise to focus on expectations. Defining the essential job functions for your department is crucial. If a faculty member cannot meet essential job functions, the chair will want to check on and discuss the provisions and policy in place to govern such things as a short leave, disability, a half-time appointment, and so on.

Even if there is no disabling factor and the faculty member says something like "But I'm just not motivated anymore," the chair will have better luck if expectations are clarified before talking about motivation. Expectations are the foundation from which a chair can have a productive interaction. The chair could say, "I'm sorry you're feeling unmotivated. Let's make sure we agree on what you're expected to do. Which parts of these expectations are the most challenging?"

*Some issues warrant special understanding, but if they have resulted in prolonged underperformance, it will still be wise to focus on expectations.*

If the faculty member is uncooperative or defiant, the chair will want to seek to understand or at least clarify the person's stance on the matter and write it down. The chair can then let the person know that the dean and others will be consulted and that there will be a follow-up meeting. The faculty member is then on notice, and the chair is on the spot to follow up. Such an in impasse is highly unlikely, however. If the chair sticks to the department's performance standards, which the dean and the legal office have approved, it should be rather easy to agree on what the faculty member is expected to do.

## ∿ Consider Ability ∿

Once Reese and Clarence had clarified expectations, Reese could then shift to *ability* and say, "Clarence, what might be getting in the way of your meeting these expectations? Do you have the resources and up-to-date skills you need? Is there any retooling that might help? How about a professional development leave? Can you see a way that the department could help?"

Reese would want to be on the lookout for any sign of feelings of inadequacy on Clarence's part, although Clarence might be reluctant to disclose them. Reese should be willing to consider whether there were resources that could be provided to help Clarence improve his skills. It's easy to confuse ability with motivation, and chairs may conclude that motivation is lacking when in fact a person's waning proficiency is actually the source of the poor performance.

## ∿ Move to Motivation ∿

Once the ability-versus-resources issue was clarified, it would be appropriate for Reese to ask Clarence about *motivation.* He might have said, "Clarence, do you *want* to meet your expectations? Is your heart in it? Do we need to consider making a change?"

Keep in mind that motivation is overwhelmingly influenced by consequences, and if Clarence said he'd like a change, Reese could consider his suggestions and would then want to consider what the consequences of such a change might be. This would take the two of them right back to discussing and clarifying the measurable expectations of a different arrangement or assignment. A part-time appointment or a leave for disability would have specific consequences and new expectations, for example.

If Clarence's performance had been atrociously deficient, Reese would probably want to initiate the three progressive steps discussed in Chapter Six. Before doing this, he would want to have discussed Clarence's performance with the dean or director of faculty relations in advance so as to benefit from their advice and to be sure he had their backing.

## ∿ Conclusion ∿

In departments where an expectations document is in place and is upheld, it doesn't matter who the chair is, who the faculty member is, or what the poor performance is about; it is, as McMillan said, essentially a matter of sitting down to discuss the gap. That's why "clarify values and expectations" is Step 1.

### Summary for Working with the Chronic Poor Performer

- Work at developing a good relationship.
- Start by clarifying and agreeing on expectations.
- Carefully visit the matter of ability; are skills or resources limiting?
- If motivation is lacking, look to make a change and clarify new expectations.
- Motivate by the application of appropriate consequences.

# CHAPTER EIGHT

# What About the Passive-Aggressive Colleague?

## Carina

*Carina was chair of the Department of Teacher Education. She was frustrated, again, with Louise. This time Louise had failed to turn in her assignment for the upcoming regional accreditation report. Carina knew that Louise didn't really buy in to the "learning outcomes fad" and wasn't all that keen on the accreditation process either. But Louise understood the department's programs as well as anyone, and it was her turn to step up and contribute.*

*Louise had actually been a mild thorn in the department's side for years. She seldom expressed her opinions in faculty meetings but would sometimes complain later about what had been decided and more than once even attempted to subvert the implementation of decisions. She had missed most of the accreditation review meetings and seemed to almost be pleased that the department might not meet its deadline.*

> *Now Carina was actually sitting down with Louise and writing the report herself, drawing out the information that only she, Louise, knew best. Carina felt like she was helping one of her children with homework. She was sure that Louise was being intentionally uncooperative. "This is demeaning to both of us," Carina thought.*

The term *passive-aggressive* (PA) is commonly used to describe people who can be frustrating, antagonistic, or even destructive in a passive way. They will accept an assignment and then fail to do it or do it late or poorly. The following are some common characteristics of PA individuals:

They procrastinate.
They resist fulfilling routine social and professional obligations.
They fail to do their share of assignments and chores.
They complain about unfairness and not being appreciated.
They are sullen or argumentative.
They blame their misfortune on others and outside factors.
They resent suggestions and reject criticism.
They criticize and scorn authority.

## ∿ Good News, Bad News ∿

The good news is that not all PA people are so deeply into their condition that they cannot be remediated. Many of us have PA tendencies. We are sometimes late for meetings and assignments. Rather than being "aggressive" and declining a task to someone's face, we accept it and then postpone following through until it's too late to do it well, and we make excuses.

It's a common defensive tactic for avoiding unpleasant jobs. Behaving this way can quite easily become a habit, but it's a habit that can be overcome.

The bad news is that there are some individuals whose passive-aggressiveness is apparently deeply rooted in some pain or grievance that they may not be able to identify or express verbally. Someone in their family may have been controlling; there may have been intense power struggles. Their emotions may be so firmly repressed that they don't even realize they're being affected by them. Their way of behaving could be self-protective. These people can be extremely difficult to work with, and succeeding with them can be so challenging that many chairs decide to not even try.

## ∿ A High-Cost Decision ∿

We can't tell if Louise is simply a work escape artist or is emotionally troubled. But if Carina chooses to continue to ignore or accommodate her, it will be a high-cost decision. Louise's weak-link behavior is diminishing the productivity of the whole department. Louise is not only failing to make her own contribution but is also penalizing Carina and the rest of the department who take up the slack. Letting Louise get away with it constitutes a reward for her bad behavior; it undermines department morale and Carina's credibility as a leader.

## ∿ Some Suggestions ∿

One survey participant chair pointed out:

> The most difficult aspect of my position is dealing with problem faculty in a way that also preserves a healthy

climate in the department overall. I've read several books, but all stop short of firm suggestions, particularly for the passive-aggressive types of problem faculty.

The following are some suggestions that might help this survey participant or any other chair to counter the destructive impact of a passive-aggressive colleague. They are my suggestions and do not constitute professional advice. They are based on the six steps covered in Part One.

## Step 1: Clarify Values and Expectations

This takes a special effort on the part of the chair and the entire department. Essential job functions should be clarified. This will likely include the number of credit hours to be taught, acceptable teaching scores, attendance in classes and availability to students, and timeliness in returning assignments, among other aspects of the job. The quantity and quality of scholarly products consistently completed will also be specified, as well as acceptable levels of service to the department and profession (see "An Expectations Document" in Chapter One).

It also takes a special effort from the chair and key supportive colleagues to be sure that each person is held to and complies with the agreed standards. Unless this is happening in Carina's department, for example, it could be impossible to persuade Louise to comply with even a simple directive.

## Step 2: Follow Policy

Even though Louise may not appear to be violating any stated policy, Carina would be wise to check. She may want to consult with the director of faculty relations and with the dean. If any PA person's aggressive behavior is severe and there's no improvement, the chair should seek professional help for what to do and whether and how to recommend that the PA person obtain help.

## Step 3: Build Trust with Colleagues

Passive-aggressive individuals usually have difficulty trusting others, and if trust is extended to them, it often backfires. They may be entangled in a web of never being forthright. If you are clear and concise in your interactions and remain consistent, they'll know what to anticipate from you—including that you expect things to improve.

Carina could call on the trust of other colleagues and engage them in assisting her by upholding expectations and supporting her in holding everyone accountable. Accountability and peer pressure combined can be effective.

## Step 4: Evaluate Yourself and Your Perceptions

Carina must be honest with herself. Is she only looking for evidence that Louise is hopeless? Does ignoring or complaining about her or doing her work for her constitute her management of the situation? If so, she may actually be contributing to the strain of the relationship and to the negative impact on the department.

Compassion has its place. Can Carina identify some personal issue Louise is struggling with? Can she think of some way she could help alleviate Louise's struggle without offloading her duties onto others?

## Step 5: Listen

As a chair, you should expect to be influenced by what you hear and see. Can you glean from your PA colleague's behavioral patterns some way that you might be able to better draw on the person's talents in a way that they are unlikely to resist?

If by listening and observing you identify an assignment that your PA colleague should be able to fulfill, make a special visit to the person's office and request his or her services. You should genuinely express your confidence in your colleague and the need for his or her skills. Pay attention to the response you get. What can you learn about what motivates this colleague? Are there clues about what else might draw the person in from the sidelines?

## Step 6: Take Effective Action

• *Recognize all the good behavior that you can.* Make sure the PA person hears your genuinely expressed appreciation for what he or she does well. A thoughtful and sincere compliment or a friendly chat about something personal can help set the stage for a productive interaction. Don't neglect to acknowledge improvement in behavior.

Carina's conversation with Louise could be encouraging and positive as she points out the benefits of everyone doing their part on time. She might say something like "I see that this goes well" and describe a positive pattern of Louise's. She could then say, "I notice you're often behind in this area," and discus the negative impact on others. Carina should ask Louise to discuss the obvious gap between her performance and what is expected of her.

• *Never ignore counterproductive behavior.* Passive-aggressive people depend on others' not noticing what they are doing. When you shine a light on their behavior, the game changes.

• *Be persistent and consistent.* Don't expect change with one meeting. Have regular interactions over a period of time using both positive feedback and evaluation of behavioral patterns. Without both persistence and consistency, it is highly unlikely that improvement will occur.

If the PA person misses a deadline, call the person on it, and if it's repeated, impose consequences.

If your PA colleague doesn't attend faculty meetings, call the person on it *every time.* Start meetings on time, and don't reward people who come late by backtracking and filling them in.

Repeatedly missing deadlines constitutes a demerit. *Do not* give a reward or a raise to encourage improvement.

A department head that I know was continually frustrated by two professors who were unfailingly late with their annual productivity reports; theirs would show up two or three weeks after the department review committee had completed reviewing everyone else's. The head, with the committee's support, announced that anyone who wanted to be considered for an annual salary increase had to turn in the report by the deadline. The head was amazed that the reports of the two professors were late again the next year. The two professors were surprised to find that their salary increases that year were zero. The following year their reports were turned in on time.

- *Use accountability minutes for meetings.* Accountability minutes consist of a record of all the decisions that are reached and all the assignments that are made. Have your assistant keep track of these as the meeting flows along. As an assignment is made, it is helpful for the chair to emphasize this by saying "So, Louise's assignment is … Louise, do you have any questions?" Whether Louise is a PA person or not, it doesn't matter; everyone is treated the same. Then again, before you leave each meeting, say, "OK, let's go over our assignments to make sure we got everything right." As your assistant reads over the minutes, clarify the date by which each assignment is due and have each person verbally commit.

When you meet again, start by going over assignments and asking for a report. Hold everyone

*Passive-aggressive people depend on others' not noticing what they are doing. When you shine a light on their behavior, the game changes.*

accountable. If someone is unprepared, say something like "Louise, we've agreed to hold each other accountable. We need your work. We're too good, and this is too important, to have it neglected." As pointed out in the discussion of PA Step 3 (above), accountability and peer pressure in combination can be effective.

• *Avoid power struggles and arguments.* Rather than debating the particulars of a single incident, point out patterns you notice in performance (in other words, build a case). Calmly point out any performance gap repetitions you see. Keep the department's expectations handy, and draw from them as needed. Make it clear that they apply to all.

• *Allow no excuses or diversions.* If the PA person makes excuses or attempts to divert the conversation to issues unrelated to the department's expectations and his or her own performance, bring the focus back to the patterns you see in the person's behavior, including repeated diversions and excuses. Say, "Let's not spend time on the particulars of the latest unmet expectation. Let's consider patterns and work out a plan for putting a stop to recurrences."

• *Probe complaints of unfairness.* If the PA person complains about the unfairness of others and blames his or her unhappiness on outside factors, keep in mind that people who question or complain about rules, policy, or the decisions of their leaders are usually attempting to excuse their own misbehavior or violation of those rules. This is of course self-destructive. See if you can work this principle into your discussion.

## Summary for Working with the Passive-Aggressive Colleague

- Do not "deal with" PA behavior by complaining about or ignoring it; this penalizes the entire department and undermines your credibility.

- Hold each person in the department to the same standards.

- Call on colleagues to help uphold standards and accountability.

- Don't accept excuses or allow diversions; focus on patterns.

- Don't expect a quick change; be persistent and consistent.

# CHAPTER NINE

# What About Bullies?

## Susan

*Susan had been chair of the Theater and Media Arts
Department for four years. She was concerned about Norman,
who had joined the department three years earlier and seemed
to be depressed. This morning she had met him in the hallway
and noticed that he resisted looking her in the eye. As she
thought about this, Susan became increasingly aware of how
she had neglected Norman. He had been hired against some
fierce opposition from three of the senior faculty who
had lobbied strongly for an alternative applicant. The three had
essentially hijacked a faculty meeting in a literal filibuster, refus-
ing to allow a conclusion until the department voted in favor
of their preferred candidate. Susan had called for a second
vote; Norman was approved.*

*The three men had since pitched their combined influence
against Norman—continually treating him either as a joke or as
if he were invisible. Susan learned that they called his student-
directed animated-film project amateurish and silly, laughing
rudely as it was shown. It haunted her that she hadn't confronted*

> *them about that. Norman's productivity and teaching were*
> *strong; she expected his record would see him successfully through*
> *to tenure and promotion. She now realized that the three "mob-*
> *sters" were apparently hoping to make his life so miserable that*
> *he'd leave before it was time to apply.*

Bullies are a challenging slice of behavior. They can be individuals or, as in this example, several people working together. They often operate behind closed doors or cloaked in the confidentiality of a group (for example, on a promotion and tenure committee). Also, most bullies work from a position of seniority or hierarchy and have learned that their prominence, rank, or connections (cronyism and schmoozing) serve as effective cover for their maneuvers.

## ∿ Applying the Six Steps to Bullying ∿

Bullies offer such a special challenge and risk that it is important to reevaluate each of the six steps with regard to bullying.

### Step 1: Clarify Values and Expectations

If Susan's department had not established any behavioral expectations, as Anna's department had (see Chapter One), she would essentially be on her own. But even a document like Anna's might have actually worked against her. Here's why. Many among us are optimists and believe that if we clarify how we all value collegiality, respect, and concern for others and that if we revisit this declaration at least annually, that will be sufficient to ensure good "citizenship" among us. Unfortunately, this very expectation of trust provides just the sort of cover under which a clever bully can thrive. This is because those who are most effectively targeted by bullies are those who prefer to avoid conflict and, when faced with discord or even intense competition, prefer to let the other guy win or simply to withdraw. Targeting a person who does his or her part to uphold a collegiality document and who trusts in the goodness of others is almost irresistible for a bully if that trusting person is doing something that threatens the bully's position or preferences.

## Step 2: Follow Policy

Odds are that Susan's university did not have a policy specifically against bullying; very few American universities do. Standard university policy to counter abusive behavior includes rules against sexual harassment and against discrimination based on gender, age, disability, religion, ethnicity, sexual orientation, and other considerations. Note that these policies protect people against "discrimination." This means that to file a claim based on these policies, a person must be able to document that he or she was treated differently than others based on gender, age, religion, or one of the other factors. If the bully is the same age or older than the victim or of the same gender and ethnicity, the victim of bullying has no legal basis for a claim. In other words, bullying is not an illegal activity.

It's typical for victims of bullying to pretend and even believe that they should be able to deal with or rise above the bullying and to deny how devastating it is to be repeatedly belittled and humiliated. But the negative effects, including high blood pressure, depression, resentment, and low self-esteem, are significant and often find their way into other areas of life and work where displaced anger or emotional absence takes a toll on fellow workers, spouses, and children. Bullying can be so damaging to the health and overall welfare of its targets that an antibullying policy is warranted. And it is possible to create and enforce policy specifically against bullying.

A sample no-bullying policy is provided in Appendix B. Note that it distinctly defines bullying and includes examples with a specificity that reaches beyond conduct that is noncollegial. It also states, similar to sexual harassment, that it is up to the person who feels that he or she is being bullied to determine the impact of the abuse, regardless of the stated intent of the perpetrator. The policy specifies consequences up to and including loss of employment. With such a policy, Susan would be in a very strong position to confront Norman's oppressors. The development of policy should be a collaborative process, based on the input and acceptance of representatives from all components of the campus, notable among them being human resources, the legal office, and students.

Note that one of the bullying-specific challenges is identifying someone at the college as the contact person (see Appendix B) for the case. Although the contact person could be someone in HR, that person will be effective only if he or she has a thorough understanding of the phenomenon of bullying, especially knowing what to look for (the occurrence of stress-related health problems, for example, and the characteristic personalities of both targets and perpetrators), and appreciates that traditional approaches to dealing with conflict can actually end up exacerbating a bullying situation rather than helping. More is said about this in following paragraphs.

## Step 3: Build Trust with Colleagues
When it comes to bullying, trust can take a traitorous twist. A chair may not be able to trust the same colleagues, at least not in the same way that he or she otherwise could, when dealing with other types of problem faculty. John Campbell says that when confronted with bullying, authority figures often "see through naughty schemes but look the other way."[1] Representatives within unions and senates may inadvertently

or intentionally protect bullies by how they choose to interpret "freedom of speech" or "contracts." Twale and De Luca note that although it is often easier for administrators to look the other way when they have other more pressing matters, doing so is unacceptable. "Perhaps," they write "leaders have no idea what to do about such problems when they encounter them because no repertoire of proven solutions exists."[2] Namie and Namie note that even the people in human resources are characteristically ineffective at handling cases of bullying, one reason being that "their primary function is management support (and 72 percent of bullies are bosses)."[3] They note that even if HR people do reach out to victims of bullying, they are likely to rely on traditional approaches to dealing with conflict and thereby actually intensify the problem. Mediation, for example, is a standard HR solution. It is designed to meet the needs of both parties, but given that bullying is a form of violence, it would be ridiculous to bring the bully together with the victim to see how the needs of each could be met. Imagine the retaliation that a dedicated and skilled bully could impose on a victim who had been asked to "work things out together." And as we have discussed, trusting that it won't happen is actually something on which bullies feed.

Although the chair is in an excellent position to observe things, these observations will be limited. Much goes on in the privacy of labs, offices, and committees where only the ground troops can witness bullying. A chair should not deny that bullying could happen in his or her department or dismiss whatever intelligence reports are received. One of the most helpful and trusting things a chair can do is to receive and openly listen to any member of the faculty or staff (or any student) who comes forward with the report of having been bullied. It takes courage for people to come forward with such information, even if they are only bystanders; thus bullying reports stand a fair chance of being valid. Of course, everything that is brought forward must be kept as confidential as possible.

## Step 4: Evaluate Yourself and Your Perceptions

A sobering observation for chairs is that bullies, in their quest to be in control and to exercise power, often seek leadership positions. Although they may not appreciate it, chairs are in a position of power. They are likely to be among the more senior members of the faculty or at least enjoy the support of senior members; otherwise they wouldn't have been selected. If the bully is among those with whom a chair hobnobs, it will be very difficult for that chair to be trusted by people outside the hobnob group, which could actually encourage bullying to thrive within that group. Unfortunately, if you tend toward bullying, you may be blind to it. Either way, you might benefit from considering how to minimize any tendency to drift that way, especially if you've recently been appointed head of a large and prominent department. Do any of the following tendencies characterize your style? If so, consider what you might do to be less intimidating and more approachable.

- You often feel that people "just don't get it" or don't appreciate your personality type.
- You prefer to interact with other administrators and leave management and operational details to others.
- Your proposals and recommendations usually go unchallenged.
- You wish other people would work as hard as you do and perform up to your high standards.
- You take full responsibility for making departmental decisions.
- You find it frustrating to work through issues or decisions with colleagues.
- You reprimand colleagues in front of others.

## Step 5: Listen

When dealing with a person who asserts that he or she has been bullied, chairs should be especially careful about listening effectively. There are few cases where it's more important to listen empathically (seeking to understand the other's emotional place) and to suppress the temptation to talk. Being understood and having his or her feelings affirmed can actually help alleviate a victim's distress. The chair should not pressure the victim to file a complaint. It is up to the victim to make that call, and if the person decides to file a formal complaint, he or she should be advised that retaliation is a virtual certainty. In spite of all that a chair might do to run interference, dedicated and practiced bullies will not fail to counter a challenge to their actions, reputation, or status.

How much should a chair listen to a bully? Depending on the severity of an incident or a history of behavior, a chair might choose to immediately enforce policy or, if there is no clear policy, to stand up to the bullying and demand that it stop. Of course, the chair would need to be careful, as noted in Chapter Four, of the natural tendency to label the other person a jerk and then go about finding yet more evidence to prove it. Just because bullying is heinous, the chair is not justified in gathering only evidence against the person accused of it. It's possible that the perceived bully is actually unaware of the impact that his or her intensity, fervor, or striving for excellence has on others. These "unconscious bullies" may be open to feedback that they are perceived as self-absorbed and insensitive and that they appear to be using others as rungs on their ladder.

When chairs attempt to offer such feedback, they should pay careful attention to the responses they encounter. If the colleague reacts with cold indifference or rude denial, even criticizing the victim in the process, the chair might want to make a written note of this as further evidence of culpability. If, on the other hand, the colleague receives the feedback openly and expresses concern and appreciation for having the matter brought to his or her attention, it could suggest that the person was truly unaware that their actions were having a negative impact on others, which would give the chair realistic hope for improvement.

## Step 6: Take Effective Action

We noted earlier that a lack of response actually serves as encouragement to those who misbehave. In the case of bullying, there's a double indemnity from failure to take action. If individuals who have been emotionally distressed reach out for help only to see that nothing is done, they have not only failed to secure relief from their suffering but are also further demeaned and dehumanized.

Unfortunately, taking effective action against bullying can be a daunting task. Where to start?

If Susan's institution did not have an antibullying policy, there would be little that Susan could use as a standard for exposing a behavioral gap if she decided to confront the threesome that were bullying Norman. Perhaps she could start now to develop antibullying policy. That would be worthwhile but would take time and strategic thinking. She would need to determine if she had support to do this, from within her department and from the dean (and on this note she probably doesn't know whether members of the three-man mob go golfing with the dean). She would want to determine whether there were any people on campus who were savvy about bullying. She might talk with other chairs and find out who the right people might be in the university senate or the faculty union. She might go online and see which institutions already have an antibullying policy and get in touch with their contact person. As in all instances of unacceptable behavior, building a case would be essential if she hoped to take action. This is where human resources could be helpful; HR might have notes in its files from previous complaints.

The authors of *Influencer* share a powerful story about bullying. In a community in South Africa, there was one citizen who upset all his neighbors by repeatedly physically abusing his wife. The people in the village felt unable to intervene, believing that a direct confrontation would be unacceptable and dangerous. They struck upon a plan. Whenever they heard the man abusing his wife, the neighbors gathered outside his front door and banged on pots and pans. What happened next was totally unexpected. Word of what the village had done spread across South African townships. Whenever spousal abuse was heard, people went and stood in front of the home where it was occurring and banged pots and pans.

The *Influencer* authors then noted, "If bad behavior is reinforced by a web of players, all the players have to be engaged in influencing change. In this particular case the neighbors had to help lead the change for good because neighbors who stood by and allowed obvious abuse to continue were a big part of the problem."[4]

Who will bang pots and pans with Susan? It's very difficult to effect cultural change in an organization where bullying has never been challenged or even discussed. If Susan were the only one to bang a pot, she could be labeled a troublemaker herself, and things could end up worse than if she had done nothing. In an ideal situation, an antibullying initiative would start at the top. Policy would be written, and discussion sessions would be held. Essential information from experienced sources would be communicated through brochures, letters, and public declarations by upper administration, then repeated by deans and chairs at regular events. Bullying awareness sessions would be made available if not mandatory. Of course, even if all essential steps and procedures were implemented, the problem of bullying (just like sexual harassment) would never disappear completely, but it could be minimized.

## ∿ A Proactive Approach ∿

There is one other proactive approach that Susan might consider. She might actually confront Norman's mob directly if she were to deploy a tactic I call "laying out extremes." To do this, she would invite the three mobsters to her office and say, "Thanks for coming to meet with me this afternoon. I called you all here because I need your help. We have a great reputation in this department, and the last thing I want is for things to fall apart on my watch. We owe our strong position in large part to the work the three of you have done over the years. I've been concerned lately about our legacy. The three of you won't be around forever. I want to make sure we're doing all we can to see that our newer generation will sustain the reputation we enjoy because of the work of stalwarts like you.

"I called you all in today to discuss what to do about Norman. We all know that the three of you were opposed to his hire. I'm not challenging that. But I'm worried. I can see at least two ways that I could screw up as chair. One way would be for me to collude with you, join you in your opposition, stack the deck against Norman, be unfair and bully him—the four of us actually becoming a mob dedicated to seeing that he fails or gets so discouraged that he leaves. That, of course, would be wrong.

"Another way I could screw up would be to oppose the three of you and your wisdom and begin defending any weaknesses Norman might have that should be corrected, enabling him and buffering him at the department's expense. That would also be a mistake.

"I want to strike the right balance. I don't want us to reject a member of our faculty that has promise and potential, and I don't want to harbor someone who is not a good fit. Either extreme would hurt our reputation for excellence and would hurt Norman."

I envision Susan standing before the group of three with a whiteboard behind her on which she has drawn a line with a midpoint. At one end she has written "mob" and at the other end she has written "enabler." Note that she has asked for help, made no accusations, clarified the potential for a mistake, and by stating extremes has made it desirable to strike a balance. If anyone from the group asks why she wrote "mob," she can define mobbing as a form of group harassment and state "That's an extreme, and we don't want to go there." Remember that she has included herself as a potential member of the mob that "we" want to avoid. If the threesome begins to dump on Norman, she can tap the line somewhere on the mobbing side of the line and say, "I'm concerned that we're off balance here." Again, she has included herself. She should ask for their suggestions and then listen, saying things like "Help me understand where you're coming from" and "What could that accomplish?"

An important point is that the issue of mobbing is out in the open and being discussed. The mob realizes that Susan is aware of what's going on and that she might well approach the dean or campus experts for further help. After visiting with these experts to ascertain their understanding of bullying, she might decide to invite them to a follow-up meeting with the mob to share their perspective. It will be an uphill battle, but at least she will have made a start.

If Susan's plight seems discouraging, that's because it is. The difficulty in dealing with bullying is a large part of what makes it so insidious. She should not overlook listening to

Norman and finding out how he would most like to proceed. Perhaps he would choose to not talk about the harassment he was receiving. That Susan is his chair and a woman might make it difficult for him to talk about whether he was experiencing any physical or emotional symptoms or whether his family was being affected. Depending on what Norman might share with her, an option that Susan should keep in mind is helping him find another job. That would constitute accepting defeat but might be much better than allowing Norman's long-term success, health, happiness, and family to be irreparably harmed.

## ∿ What If the Bully Is a Student? ∿

The problem of university students bullying faculty is apparently widespread. Audrey June reports that "most professors can recount a moment when students have been excessively rude, threatened them, or even made them fear physical violence."[5] She tells the story of one female associate professor who counts on at least one student each semester to "push the limits of classroom civility and the professor-student relationship."

June reports that women faculty members are affected disproportionately, with one-third of them experiencing a very serious confrontation that caused them to fear for their physical well-being; one-fifth of male professors had similar experiences. The article was followed by a collection of comments identifying actions that those in higher education have found most helpful for dealing with student bullies. A frequent first step was to set the right tone at the start. "I have taken the bull by the horns,"

*This kind of behavior really does happen, but it's not going to happen in your class.*

reported one professor, "... by placing material on my syllabus that addresses this kind of behavior. So far it has helped. Let me encourage all to deal with this issue on the first day of class. Some people will wonder why you're doing so, but you can tell them, this kind of behavior really does happen, but it's not going to happen in your class."

Other helpful comments included the following:

- "Confront student bullying immediately." If this is not done, the bully wins while the professor loses the respect of the rest of the students, and incivility and rudeness usually remain a problem throughout the semester. Many professors regretted being lenient and not having the student removed from the class permanently.

- "Be respectful." This not only consisted of being considerate of students but also included being mindful of the power differential between professors and students and the propensity of some professors to be bullies themselves. Confronting bad behavior with an invitation to meet after class and then listening to discover the student's frustrations was recommended.

- "Quickly involve the right people" to ensure that policy is followed and that the student is provided due process.

Although it's usually an automatic response to inform the department chair or dean of such behavior, most professors found this to be unhelpful or even a mistake. Many reported that their chair and dean not only didn't know what to do but tended to think less of the professor because he or she was having problems in class. Contacting the dean of students was the most frequently recommended step. The dean of students and his or her office are experienced in dealing with student issues, and in the majority of cases, faculty who worked with them were appreciative of the actions taken and the help they received.

Rather than defaulting to the dean of students to deal with classroom bullying, it seems that we as chairs ought to make sure that any professor who approaches us with concerns about belligerent in-class behavior isn't automatically judged to be a problem teacher.

## ∿ What If the Bully Is Your Boss? ∿

This scary scenario summons up comments from three experts with different backgrounds and perspectives. C. K. Gunsalus is an attorney and professor who served as associate provost at the University of Illinois; she teaches leadership and ethics. Robert Sutton is a professor in the Department of Management Science and Engineering at Stanford University; he researches evidence-based management. Joseph Grenny is coauthor of four *New York Times* best sellers; he is cofounder of VitalSmarts, a corporate training group. Quotes from the publications of these three follow.

Gunsalus's recommendation for dealing with a bullying boss may seem pessimistic; she would likely say it constitutes reality and a strategy for self-preservation:

> If what you perceive as inappropriate or unprofes-
> sional bullying is directed primarily or solely at you,
> and it's severe, not something you can grin and bear,
> your best bet is probably to cut your losses and leave. If
> you're isolated in that kind of situation, unless the bully
> is very near the end of his or her career, the costs to you
> from staying are likely to be vastly disproportionate to the
> benefits, no matter how strong your commitment to
> the institution. This is especially the case if your bête noir
> is relatively recently appointed and basking in official favor.

If the problem is more widely shared and/or acknowledged, you still must exercise great care and caution, and should still consider whether you'd be better off leaving. The nature of authority in organizations means that you're facing an uphill battle in which you may well come to be seen as the problem. There are constructive steps that can be taken, but they are far beyond the scope of this book and require an ongoing delicate calculus, the essence of which, at every turn, must be whether it's more costly to you to persevere than to move on.[6]

Sutton is only slightly less pessimistic. If standing up to the bully is not a viable option for you, he recommends finding spaces and occasions where you can hide or counter, perhaps by going out of your way to be supportive of others (which could include students). "But," he says "detached indifference, simply not giving a damn, might be the best that you can do to survive a workplace that subjects you to relentless humiliation."[7] He also says that finding other victims, if they exist, and sharing feelings and experiences with them might be helpful.

But talking with other people about your problems isn't a panacea. . . . I've found that conversations, gossip sessions, and even therapy sessions led by professionals sometimes do more harm than good. These gatherings sometimes degenerate into 'bitch sessions' where victims complain bitterly about how bad things are and how powerless they are to stop it.[8]

Sutton agrees with Gunsalus when he points out that attempting to adapt to bullying has a dark side. It "might provide just enough protection (or, worse yet, fuel just enough delusion of protection) to stop people from bailing out of relentlessly demeaning situations—even when they have exit options."[9]

Grenny has more optimistic counsel, but his advice centers on interacting with a powerful boss who tends to be defensive rather than with an unmitigated bully. He writes that "bosses will listen to just about anyone who is skilled at making them feel safe" and that "there are two special considerations in making bosses feel safe" (the wording that follows is a summary):

- You must show that you respect both your boss as well as his or her position.
- You must assure your boss that you are committed to his or her goals.

"When bosses get defensive (or anyone for that matter)," Grenny concludes, "it is generally because you have failed to assure them on one or both of these two points."[10]

I have never been victimized by an out-and-out bully, but I've witnessed it happening to others. I'm not a psychologist, but I sense that the inner damage of intense bullying goes much deeper and persists much longer than most of us can appreciate. In this regard I can agree with Gunsalus and Sutton, who recommend cutting your losses and leaving. If taking a different job means disrupting the schooling of your children or your spouse's job, I would deliberate with them and other important stakeholders, consider the options, and be prepared to deep-six the existing situation, move on, and celebrate being free from the kind of mistreatment that no one ever deserves.

# Summary for Dealing with Bullies

Even if you don't have a problem with bullying in your department, consider establishing antibullying policy. This is most effective if it's institutional rather than departmental.

- Regularly revisit and uphold your policies on civility and bullying. Make it clear that bullying and incivility are not tolerated in your unit.

- Be on the lookout for signs of bullying; don't assume it could not happen in your department.

- Be open and receptive to anyone (including students) who might approach you with claims or concerns regarding bullying. Make it safe for them to talk with you.

- Recognize that chairs can be bullies and are often prone to wink at bullying, especially if the perpetrator is an influential or favored colleague.

- Keep in mind that conventional approaches to dealing with problem faculty are often ineffective for dealing with bullies; it takes special experience and training to appreciate the nuances of the bully culture and to know what to do about it.

- Understand that removing a bully without changing the social order only creates a vacancy for the next one.

## Notes

1. J. Campbell. (2000). *Dry rot in the ivory tower* (p. 31). Lanham, MD: University Press of America.

2. D. Twale & B. De Luca. (2008). *Faculty incivility: The rise of the academic bully culture and what to do about it* (p. 22). San Francisco: Jossey-Bass.

3. G. Namie & R. F. Namie. (2011). *The bully-free workplace: Stop jerks, weasels, and snakes from killing your organization* (p. 129). Hoboken, NJ: Wiley.

4. K. Patterson, J. Grenny, D. Maxfield, R. McMillan, & A. Switzler. (2008). *Influencer: The power to change anything* (p. 180). New York: McGraw-Hill.

5. A. W. June. (2010, August 1). When students become class bullies, professors are among the victims. *The Chronicle of Higher Education.* Retrieved from http://chronicle.com/article/When-Students-Become-Class/123733/

6. C. K. Gunsalus. (2006). *The college administrator's survival guide* (p. 136). Cambridge, MA: Harvard University Press.

7. R. I. Sutton. (2007). *The no asshole rule: Building a civilized workplace and surviving one that isn't* (p. 138). New York: Warner Business Books.

8. R. I. Sutton. (2007). *The no asshole rule: Building a civilized workplace and surviving one that isn't* (p. 146). New York: Warner Business Books.

9. R. I. Sutton. (2007). *The no asshole rule: Building a civilized workplace and surviving one that isn't* (p. 157). New York: Warner Business Books.

10. J. Grenny. (2007, September 26)). Crucial conversations with your boss. *Crucial Skills Newsletter, 5*(39). Retrieved from http://www.vitalsmarts.com/userfiles/File/newsletter/Newsletter092607QA.html

## CHAPTER TEN

# What About the Problem Characters Who Emerge During Times of Change?

## David

*David had been dean of the College of Arts and Sciences for four years. The college was in the midst of a reinvention. Whole departments had been dismantled and new ones formed, some out of pieces of three previous units. The college curriculum had been reduced by one-third. Satellite units had been closed. One of David's fellow deans from a different college shared his impression that "this is the sort of thing that results in earthquakes and suicides."*

*When David had come to the college from another university, a friend back home, who had himself been a dean, said, "Now remember, David, the last thing you ever want to do is reorganize. Just go down there and preside. Show up at events. Promote the goodness in people. Help them celebrate. Enjoy yourself." David had intended to follow that advice, but university demographics and budget cuts had led him to "preside" over the very thing that he had been both warned against and determined to avoid. Chaos and trauma resulting from the reinvention were high when David was presented with a collection of sixteen letters of protest from college faculty; all but two were unsigned, and the majority asked for his resignation.*

*"David, my boy," the academic vice president said, "you've really done it, haven't you. You've got them all riled up; they're polarized in a manner we've never seen at this university before. I've a mind to honor the request made by this stack of ugly letters and ask you to resign."*

Next to dealing with problem faculty, guiding change was the survey item chairs most wanted help with.[1] It's no surprise that both challenges often coincide, and in a manner that can be devastating to faculty, chairs, and the staff. The fact is that chairs cannot avoid change, which sometimes produces the level of trauma that David was experiencing. The literature consistently points out that the department chair is the primary change agent within the university. Ann Lucas and colleagues declare that "the department is the place from which change needs to be launched, and ... the chair is the right person to lead such change."[2] Don Chu writes, "Central administrators can preach the need for change in the institution, but it is at the department level where change must take place."[3]

Accepting the inevitability of change does not alter the fact that it will be traumatic—resisted by some and accompanied by risk, trauma, and loss for many. This chapter focuses on the challenging characters that typically emerge when change is traumatic, why they often prove challenging, and what an administrator can do to minimize the associated distress.

## ∽ Change Cycles and Change Characters ∽

Everett Rogers spent his career in academia studying how people respond to innovation. He researched hundreds of situations where people were confronted with change and documented how a normal population of humans typically responds, whether confronted with an innovation such as taking limes on board British ships to combat scurvy (clear apparent advantage), to fluoridation of water (controversial). Other examples included farmers adopting hybrid corn, or children buying hand-held video games. Rogers is known for his normal distribution curve showing that the majority (68 percent) of people fall within one standard deviation of the mean, with half (34 percent) constituting an "early majority" (innovate quickly) and half a "late majority."[4] Beyond one standard deviation are 13.5 percent (including some leaders) whom Rogers called "early adopters," and at the other end 16 percent called "laggards" who resist or obstruct change. Two standard deviations away from the mean, and within the early adopter group, Rogers placed 2 percent of people called "innovators."

Phillip Schlechty uses more colloquial labels to describe what he calls the "five types of actors" who engage in any change endeavor.[5] I have imposed Schlechty's descriptions onto a normal distribution with one and two standard deviations from the mean (following Rogers's example) to produce Figure 10.1 (the division of "settlers" into early settlers and late settlers is my wording, not Schlechty's). Schlechty did not assign percentages to his groups. He preferred to not directly equate "trailblazers" to Rogers's "innovators"; he felt that

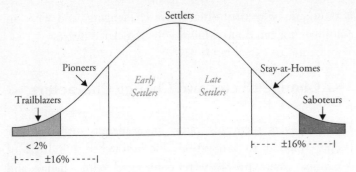

**Figure 10.1** Change characters according to Phillip Schlechty

trailblazers were rarer than 2 percent of the population. He said that about 16 percent of a population's being pioneers was reasonable.

Not surprisingly, it is the members of the group located on the fringes of the normal population that most often turn out to be the problem faculty during times of change. Knowing about them and their inclinations can help an administrator exploit their constructive tendencies and minimize their destructive impact. The following discussions are based on Schlechty's character labels, and unless indicated otherwise all quotes are his.[6]

## Trailblazers

These change characters are rare and valuable. They are willing to trek into unchartered territory all alone. They thrive on freedom and newness and may or may not have a vision of where they're going or what they intend to do when they get there. There are several things a chair can do to take advantage of a trailblazer's gifts and keep them from becoming problematic. First, the chair must constantly remind the trailblazer that he or she belongs to a community and should help link the person's vision to that of the department, college, and university. Second, the chair should know that trailblazers desire to be commended for their boldness, even applauded.

> Trailblazers are needed, but they are not easy to live with in the sedate environments of committee meetings and seminar rooms. . . . And leaders are not doing their job if they do not seek every opportunity to put local trailblazers out in front, including helping them write proposals to get support for their work and proposals that will permit them to share their work at conferences.

Sally Kuhlenschmidt suggests using the term *mountain men* instead of *trailblazers* because of their tendency to be genuine loners operating beyond the limits of convention.[7] She notes that they can be easily distracted, may jump the gun, and have a problem with long-term planning and supervision.[8]

As long as a chair is aware of what a trailblazer looks like and what his inclinations and needs are, his talents can be anything but a problem. A common challenge is that the chair too might lean toward being a late settler or even a stay-at-home. If you are confronted with a need to change and are lucky enough to have a trailblazer in your unit, build trust with that person and draw on (and channel) his or her inspiration.

## Pioneers

According to Schlechty, pioneers are like trailblazers—"an adventurous and hardy lot who are willing to take considerable risks." Pioneers and trailblazers often feed off of each other. A difference between trailblazers and pioneers is that pioneers have a considerable need for assurance that the upcoming change will be beneficial. Here's where a little homework on the part of the chair can be helpful. Much of the literature on dealing with change notes that if a department is successful in effecting transformation, it must have a clear vision of what it wants to look like in the future and an agreed mission to clarify its most important purposes. With these in place, it can confidently welcome the winds of change and modify itself to match its vision and purpose.

> "On guiding department change, it's amazing how changes fail to register with long-term colleagues. One must prepare them for the possibility, take them through the discussion carefully, and create a very clear 'paper' record after the fact."
>
> —*Survey comment*

David Whetten and Kim Cameron offer some practical advice on getting ready for change:

> One way to create readiness for change is to compare current levels of performance to the highest standards you can find. Identifying who else performs at spectacular levels helps set a standard toward which people can aspire. It identifies a target of opportunity. This is referred to as benchmarking, and it involves finding best practice, studying it in detail, and then planning to exceed that performance.[9]

Don Chu suggests approaching benchmarking by asking several questions:

> What is the best department that you know? What makes it so good? Is it distinctive in some way? What would have

to be done to your department to emulate the best department you know? What does the best department you know of feel like in the halls? What is its climate like? . . . How does your budget look compared to that exemplary department's budget? . . . How is performance counseling handled? How much professional development goes on there? . . . What would a chair have to do to make his or her own department the best teaching department on campus?[10]

Keep in mind that early-adopting pioneers are generally well respected and looked up to. It is therefore essential that the chair include pioneers in discussions around the kinds of questions Chu asks. Pioneers should also be deployed in communicating the change vision. As a note of caution, Kuhlenschmidt points out that pioneers may be prone to jump to a new project before finishing an existing one and, like trailblazers, may resist supervision.[11]

## Settlers

Settlers want to know what to expect. They like detailed maps and guidebooks and prefer to make reservations before they depart.

Schlechty points out:

> Perhaps the most critical thing to remember about settlers is that they need strong, constant, and reassuring leadership that inspires them to keep going when they are tempted to turn back. Those who would work with settlers must understand that systemic change does not make things better or easier in the short run; instead, it is likely to create uncertainty, doubt, and confusion.[12]

Keep in mind that Schlechty did not assign percentages to any of the groups, but settlers do constitute the bulk of the "normal" members of a group. The needs of this 68 percent majority cannot be overlooked while focusing on the demands or problematic tendencies of those on the fringes. On the other hand, I have interacted with some academic administrators who believe it is not productive to "waste time" catering to the whims of outliers and focus only on members of the faculty who reside within the norm.

Schlechty notes that settlers will notice what he calls an "implementation dip," which is a natural part of change. He says, "The old way of doing things, although perhaps not as good as the new way, has one advantage: it is familiar and people know how to do it. The new way is unfamiliar and requires learning and practice."[13]

We've all experienced the implementation dip. Think of a simple personal change like adopting new writing software. Until we get used to it and discover its advantages, we experience discouraging downtime. Or consider remodeling a home. When the plumbing is out and we have to go to the service station down the street to use the bathroom and Mother is crying amid the sawdust and chaos, it's hard to convince the kids that it really will be better soon. It is helpful not just for the settlers but also for everyone else to have their change leaders identify benchmarks of progress and not only note and celebrate when they are met but also point out what to look for next.

A chair cannot overcommunicate during times of change. An administrator once counseled me that you have not communicated your message until it has been delivered ten times and in ten different ways. You should deliver it orally to large groups, to small groups, and one-on-one. You should send it out on hard copy. You should e-mail it. You should have someone else also deliver it. You should solicit feedback and then meet with the large and small groups again and show that they have been heard and how you have responded. Another hard copy and e-mail should follow. You can make posters, you can use newsletters, and you can send fliers. And after all this, there will still be some who will say, "Why didn't somebody tell us about this?"

## Stay-at-Homes

Schlechty points out that "people who do not respond enthusiastically, or at least compliantly, to the desires of change leaders are often viewed as problems, and unfortunately, for the change process, such problems get attention."[14] He advises chairs not to spend too much energy worrying over the reluctance or resistance of stay-at-homes. Better to accept the fact that they may never endorse the new way.

It is my opinion that in a collegial department, laggards and stay-at-homes can be respected and perhaps even honored for the valuable role they play in dealing with change. They often provide helpful balance for a department that may be moving too quickly toward the cusp of untested transformation. The truth is that much of what appears to be resistance to change turns out to be just plain good sense. If laggards (quite often the older members of a group) are treated with respect and if their wisdom is solicited, chances are that because they feel understood and valued, they will avoid aligning themselves with saboteurs even if they won't embrace the change.

Ron Heifetz writes:

> The pains of change deserve respect. People can only sustain so much loss at any one time. Leadership demands respect for people's basic need for direction, protection, and order in times of distress. Leadership requires compassion for the distress of adaptive change, both because compassion is its own virtue and because it can improve one's sense of timing. Knowing how hard to push and when to let up are central to leadership.[15]

Sally Kuhlenschmidt points out that some stay-at-homes would really like to be pioneers but cannot because of circumstance.[16] In the context of settling America, perhaps they stayed back east because they had aging parents who needed their care or similar commitments that prevented them from pulling up stakes. This metaphor could represent a variety of professional obligations that handicap academics, depending on timing. Chairs should also be mindful of individuals who may be caught in emotional or psychological challenges during a period of change; to these people, change, especially sudden change, can be the straw that breaks the back of their emotional stability. It is essential that these individuals be given plenty of notice well in advance, perhaps with some handholding by understanding and trusted colleagues.

## Saboteurs

People who actively engage in obstructing change might be viewed as hooligans or mutineers because of their tactics. Schlechty points out that the most effective saboteurs have many qualities and needs that are strikingly similar to those of trailblazers: they are often "lone rangers" willing to take risks. Saboteurs can be quite disruptive and may not be willing to state their concerns openly. They should never be ignored or left on the outside, where their disruptive work may go undetected. Instead the chair should try to co-opt them by inviting them to participate in change discussions, listening to what they say and perhaps even assigning them a part. Certainly saboteurs can be disruptive, and some will not cooperate enough to communicate their concerns. However, if change leaders continue to reach out to all resisters and critics and try hard to understand them, the leaders will often learn a great deal.

## ◦ Returning to David ◦

As it turns out, there were 103 faculty members in David's reinvented college. Assuming his was a "normal" college, he should therefore have expected sixteen of his faculty to be positioned on each "side" of the change taking place (half being trailblazers and pioneers, very likely to favor the reform, and half being stay-at-homes or even saboteurs, aligned firmly against it).

How much better would David and the rest of the college leadership have weathered their change experience had they known that sixteen obstructionists out of hundred were to be expected? This is not to say that David should have ignored those sixteen. Instead he would have been wise to go out of his way to engage them, to listen to them, to be sure that they felt understood. Perhaps he could have better acknowledged the losses the entire college was feeling. The reality is, however, that doing all of this thoroughly might not have changed very many sentiments. Heifetz noted that "one often cannot shield oneself from the outrage of those parties who must face loss and are unwilling to change."[17]

## ◦ A Caveat ◦

The groups proposed by Rogers and Schlechty are stereotypes, and any application to individuals should be approached with sensitivity and caution. Kuhlenschmidt notes that individuals may actually portray different character types in different periods of their life or assignments (think chair versus independent faculty member). She also points out that while trailblazers and pioneers may interact comfortably, pairing trailblazers with stay-at-homes on a change enterprise without a skilled moderator may be ruinous.[18] Whatever types of characters you are surrounded with and no matter what type of change you face, you will be wise to clarify the unit's values and expectations, follow policy, build trust, evaluate yourself and your perceptions, listen, and then take effective action. Consider Yogi Berra's advice: "When you come to a fork in the road, take it!"[19]

## Summary for Dealing with the Problem Characters Who Emerge During Times of Change

- Expect that change will energize some people and traumatize others; polarized reactions are normal and do not indicate that things have gone wrong.

- Consider how to effectively interact with and utilize the strengths of each of the character types in your group; don't attempt to persuade the majority to see things your way.

- Have an agreed mission, and help all characters link their vision or perspective to it.

- Prepare for a little chaos while in the midst of change and for a little down time as the group adjusts to the new way.

- Communicate, communicate, communicate; identify benchmarks of progress.

- Accept the fact that some members of any normal group will never be supportive.

## Notes

1. R. K. Crookston. (2010). Results from a national survey: The help chairs want most. *The Department Chair, 21*(1), 13–15.

2. A. F. Lucas & Associates. (2000). *Leading academic change: Essential roles for department chairs* (p. 2). San Francisco: Jossey-Bass.

3. D. Chu. (2006). *The department chair primer: Leading and managing academic departments* (p. 118). Bolton, MA: Anker.

4. E. M. Rogers. (2003). *Diffusion of innovations* (5th ed., pp. 280–285). New York: Free Press.

5. P. C. Schlechty. Personal communication, April 17, 2009.

6. P. C. Schlechty. (1997). *Inventing better schools* (pp. 210–211). San Francisco: Jossey-Bass.

7. S. Kuhlenschmidt, personal communication, November 22, 2010.

8. S. Kuhlenschmidt. (2001). *Theory of teacher adaptation to change.* Retrieved from http://people.wku.edu/sally.kuhlenschmidt /presentation/plantingseeds/typology.htm

9. D. A. Whetten & K. S. Cameron. (2007). *Developing management skills* (7th ed.; p. 556). Upper Saddle River, NJ: Pearson Prentice Hall.

10. D. Chu. (2006). *The department chair primer: Leading and managing academic departments* (pp. 115–116). Bolton, MA: Anker.

11. S. Kuhlenschmidt. (2001). *Theory of teacher adaptation to change.* Retrieved from http://people.wku.edu/sally.kuhlenschmidt /presentation/plantingseeds/typology.htm

12. P. C. Schlechty. (1997). *Inventing better schools* (p. 215). San Francisco: Jossey-Bass.

13. P. C. Schlechty. (1997). *Inventing better schools* (p. 215). San Francisco: Jossey-Bass.

14. P. C. Schlechty. (1997). *Inventing better schools* (p. 217). San Francisco: Jossey-Bass.

15. R. A. Heifetz. (1994). *Leadership without easy answers* (p. 241). Cambridge, MA: Harvard University Press.

16. S. Kuhlenschmidt, personal communication, November 22, 2010.

17. R. A. Heifetz. (1994). *Leadership without easy answers* (p. 240). Cambridge, MA: Harvard University Press.

18. S. Kuhlenschmidt. (2001). *Theory of teacher adaptation to change.* Retrieved from http://people.wku.edu/sally.kuhlenschmidt /presentation/plantingseeds/typology.htm

19. Y. Berra. (2001). *When you come to a fork in the road, take it!* New York: Hyperion.

# CHAPTER ELEVEN

# What About the Psychologically Impaired?

*Carolyn Oxenford and*
*Sally Kuhlenschmidt*

Carolyn Oxenford is a professor of psychology and director of the Center for Teaching Excellence at Marymount University, Washington, D.C.; she earned a Ph.D. in clinical psychology from Emory University. Sally Kuhlenschmidt is a professor of psychology and director of the Faculty Center for Excellence in Teaching at Western Kentucky University in Bowling Green; she earned a Ph.D. in clinical psychology from Purdue University.

# Lawrence

*Lawrence was agonizing over what to do about Marian, one of the most energetic yet most aggravating members of his faculty. Before she joined the faculty, Marian had a long history with the department, first as an undergraduate student and then as a secretary and graduate student. She had always been regarded as a creative and passionate advocate for her discipline and for students, but over the first three years of her employment as a faculty member, her behavior had shifted from creative to "flighty." At first her problems seemed to be health-related as she went from one physical challenge to the next, but even in the interim between hospitalizations Marian's work was disorganized, capricious, and unreliable, and she seemed to veer from crisis to crisis. Students complained about lost papers, erratic grading, and missed classes, even though they loved the time she spent with them exploring ideas. Lawrence suspected that she contributed to her repeated crises by not anticipating the effect of her poor choices. Mentoring had not helped, and her faculty colleagues were tired of fixing her crises. Lawrence had held several disciplinary meetings with her and was contemplating yet another, which he sensed might consist of serving her with a notice of termination. What bothered Lawrence deeply was that he didn't know if Marian was just a disorganized prima donna whose behavior should not be tolerated or if she were struggling with some kind of psychological problem that impaired her ability to function effectively in the faculty role.*

According to the most recent National Comorbidity Survey, more than 25 percent of American adults experienced the symptoms of a diagnosable mental disorder over the course of a year.[1] For more than half of those individuals, the symptoms were considered either moderate or serious, a level of impairment that would have a noticeable effect on daily job functioning. The same survey estimated that over their lifetimes, approximately 50 percent of Americans will qualify for a diagnosis of some type of mental disorder. David Schwebel found similar levels of impairment among faculty, estimating rates of mental illness of approximately 20 percent to 25 percent in that group.[2]

Research from Australia,[3] the United Kingdom,[4] and the United States[5] suggests that psychological distress occurs more frequently in academic professionals than in the general population. This may be in part because individuals who are attracted to academic careers have characteristics that predispose them to developing psychological symptoms. For example, faculty members may experience maladaptive perfectionism, defined as "punishing and unattainable standards that reflect an inadequate sense of self and that can lead to unyielding self-criticism and an inability to experience pleasure through normal accomplishments."[6]

*Psychological distress occurs more frequently in academic professionals than in the general population.*

Department chairs should expect to encounter colleagues whose mental health negatively affects their performance at work. Ignoring these issues can result in a range of negative outcomes, including the loss of a gifted faculty member and lowered departmental morale progressing to litigation if the situation is mishandled. Recognizing when mental health issues may be part of the problem and how best to work with colleagues whose work-related issues are rooted in mental health concerns is unfortunately a skill that few chairs possess.

## ∿ Recognizing Mental Health Issues ∿

A mental health disorder is essentially a constellation of extreme variations on common behaviors. These patterns of behavior reach the level of disorder when they actively interfere with a person's ability to function effectively or to experience positive emotions. For example, Professor A forgets to return papers or misplaces them but eventually grades them accurately and returns them late in the semester. Students are annoyed but not excessively harmed. This is not good practice and causes students to complain, but they do receive their feedback eventually and are able to complete the course. Compare this to Professor B, who never hands the papers back at all or hands them back with seemingly random comments. Students complain and are harmed by not receiving meaningful feedback on their work. Something is impairing Professor B's ability to function in his job, although we cannot know yet if it is related to some type of mental impairment. All of the behaviors we describe in this chapter exist on a continuum, and many of us find variations on our own behaviors among the signs and symptoms of mental disorder; it is the particular type of symptoms, their severity, and the functional impairments that define a disorder and cause concern. Faculty members who show many signs of disordered behavior or extreme levels of dysfunction may need to be referred to a mental health professional.

Examples of specific faculty behavior that may suggest a mental health problem are provided in Appendix C.

## ∿ Using the Six Steps to Work Effectively with Psychologically Impaired Colleagues ∿

Let's revisit Marian's behavior. Her pattern of disorganized and extremely irritating behavior and the complaints by students and colleagues suggest that she may be struggling with a psychological impairment, such as attention deficit disorder or an anxiety disorder. If Lawrence had thought this might be the case, what should his next steps be? How might he apply the six-step process to Marian's situation and achieve a positive resolution?

### Step 1: Clarify Values and Expectations

Step 1 involves examining the context of your department and university. There are wide variations between colleges and universities in what constitutes appropriate faculty behavior. Even within a single institution, individual departments may have dramatically different behavioral norms. For example, behavior that is considered merely eccentric in one academic environment may be viewed much more negatively in another. In a highly tolerant department, faculty with mental health issues may continue to function and openly display unusual behaviors. This type of environment may be so forgiving and accepting of faculty mental health issues that problems can escalate dramatically before anyone is willing to confront them. In such a setting, Marian's behavior might have been overlooked until it was too extreme to correct.

Low-tolerance departments are less supportive of faculty with mental health issues; even mildly unusual behavior may be viewed as a sign of weakness that might lead to a loss of resources or respect or provide grounds for disciplinary action. This type of climate may discourage innovation and creativity and encourage faculty to hide their problems. If you are wondering why a faculty member with an obvious problem seems isolated and does not confide in anyone, consider your departmental climate; reticence may be a very appropriate response to the situation. In Marian's case, both students and faculty were complaining about her behavior, so it is likely that she had violated departmental behavioral norms, but that does not necessarily mean she could not function as a faculty member elsewhere. Would her behavior be severe enough to prevent her from being successful in your department? What are your department's expectations in the areas of grading timeliness and accuracy, managing student work, and collegiality? Clarifying departmental values and expectations will help define the boundary between individuality and mental disorder, between success and termination. Then you as the department chair will be in a better position to determine whether a colleague has crossed that boundary. If your departmental boundaries seem to be on either of the extreme ends of the tolerance continuum, you may want to consider the potential impact of your departmental culture on the well-being of your faculty and the productivity of your department.

Ambiguity is a stressor for everyone. Clearly specified departmental values and expectations are particularly critical when managing faculty with psychological impairments. Persons with mental health disorders in general will perform better with some degree of structure. If your department does not have clearly defined behavioral outcomes for productivity, civility, and decorum, it will be difficult to evaluate whether faculty members are achieving required outcomes.

It may also become difficult to identify the essential job functions that all members of the faculty must be able to perform, which are key to applying the provisions of the Americans with Disabilities Act (discussed in Step 2). It may be particularly tough to define what is outside the boundary in highly tolerant departments. Conversely, in a department with very low levels of tolerance, it may be difficult to propose accommodations that are reasonable but fall outside the department's behavioral norms. How was Marian introduced to the departmental norms? Did the mentoring Marian received help her meet departmental expectations for productivity, civility, and decorum, or were mentors unable to articulate those departmental norms or guide her behavior? What sort of mentoring and socialization into departmental culture happens in your department?

## Step 2: Follow Policy

Before you can follow policy with regard to managing psychologically impaired faculty, you need to know what that policy is; in some cases, you may need to develop it. In addition to general policies on appropriate behavior and conduct, when dealing with psychologically impaired faculty, policy also includes understanding the Americans with Disabilities Act (ADA; ada.gov) (or laws appropriate to your country) and how your university implements its provisions.

The goal of the ADA is to prevent discrimination against disabled individuals. It also seeks to ensure a work environment that permits employers to fully benefit from all of their employee's skills. Having a general understanding of the ADA will help you work with any type of disabled faculty member; however, we will focus on issues related to mental health disabilities specifically. These issues include defining mental health disabilities and essential job functions and understanding the employer's responsibilities in accommodating disabled individuals.

### Defining Disability

The ADA defines disability as any impairment that "substantially limits performance of a major life activity" [Sec. 1630.2(g) (1)(i), Code of Federal Regulations].[7] Mental impairments may be disabling conditions and are defined as "an intellectual disability (formerly termed 'mental retardation'), organic brain syndrome, emotional or mental illness, and specific learning disabilities" [Sec. 1630.2(h)(2)]. The criteria for classifying a mental condition as disabling do not take into account the impact of ameliorating treatments such as medication or psychotherapy. For example, if an individual who suffers from schizophrenia cannot perform essential job functions without medication, the person would be considered disabled under the ADA even if able to perform his or her duties while medicated. However, if an individual has been diagnosed with schizophrenia, is not taking medication, and does not show substantial limitations of a major life activity, the person is not considered disabled under the ADA. Diagnosis alone is not enough.

Some qualifications exist in the definitions of allowable disabling conditions. Whereas alcohol abuse can be considered a disabling condition by the ADA, abuse of illegal or controlled substances is specifically excluded, as are gender identity disorders, sexual behavior disorders, kleptomania, pyromania, and compulsive gambling (Sec. 1630.3). Individuals who are in recovery from any type of substance abuse can be considered to have a disabling condition if performance of major life activities is affected by the condition.

### Essential Job Functions

If a faculty member has a disabling mental health condition and can perform "essential job functions" (as defined by the university), the ADA requires the university to make reasonable accommodations that would allow the employee to succeed on the job. Defining the essential job functions for your department is critical because you cannot apply different standards to disabled and nondisabled faculty. Is coming to class on time and avoiding frequent absences essential for everyone? What about maintaining rational and civil relationships with colleagues and students? *Defining the essential job functions for your department is critical.* This is where the campus code of conduct and clear departmental expectations are necessary. If rude outbursts, chronic lateness, or canceling classes is overlooked in other faculty, it is highly unlikely that these would qualify as essential job functions. The ADA can support the department chair who is committed to helping faculty manage mental health issues, but only if the department has clearly defined and consistently applied standards for faculty behavior that respect academic freedom while still expecting civil behavior.

### Employer Responsibilities and Exceptions

Once an individual has been determined to be disabled under the ADA, employers are required to provide reasonable accommodations. Reasonable accommodations might include scheduling changes, moving an office or class to a less distracting environment, or providing more structured supervision. Accommodations that cause undue hardship for the employer are not required. Eliminating teaching assignments altogether for a faculty member or limiting contact with colleagues or students would quite certainly be considered to cause undue hardship.

ADA regulations also state that employers may take action against an employee who poses a direct threat in the workplace regardless of the person's status. They define "direct threat" as "a significant risk of substantial harm to the health or safety of the individual or others that cannot be eliminated or reduced by reasonable accommodation" [Sec. 1630.2(r)]. The university must identify specific behaviors that pose the direct threat. A psychologically impaired individual is not a direct threat merely because he or she has a history of psychiatric problems. Threatening or intimidating colleagues or students is the most likely evidence of direct threat you are likely to experience as a department chair. Barbara Lee and Peter Ruger provide a more detailed overview of ADA issues in higher education settings.[8]

To claim ADA protection, faculty members must disclose details about their disability to the university. Faculty members may choose not to disclose their status for many valid reasons, including loss of privacy and fear of social stigmatization. The decision to disclose a disability is one that you cannot help faculty members make if you have supervisory responsibilities toward them, but they need to be aware of the advantages and disadvantages of their choice. Understanding the specific policies and processes at your university will allow you to make appropriate referrals to someone who can support faculty members as they consider their options. These policies and processes vary widely, depending on the extent of prior planning the institution has done to manage mental health disability issues and the size of the institution (a large university may have a dedicated ADA officer, whereas smaller schools may have very little in the way of support). If no clear procedures exist, you may need to raise this concern with your human resources office or dean.

Marian's case was particularly complex, as there were physical health issues as well as interrelated behavioral problems. Lawrence felt that Marian's behaviors clearly fell outside of departmental standards and warranted action, and yet he found no evidence of direct threat or dangerous behavior. Marian did not disclose any mental health issues to Lawrence; however, he felt that self-sabotage was a contributing factor in her unproductive behavior. Self-sabotage can occur in a number of mental health problems as a cry for help. Marian's campus had an ADA officer, but only recently had it adopted a plan for employee ADA needs, including an online employee assistance program. Many persons did not know it was available, and Marian was not the sort of person to use online resources. Did Marian really have meaningful access to an

ADA officer and information about whether she was eligible for ADA accommodations? Had Lawrence arranged for her to meet with an ADA officer or an employee assistance provider? Does such support exist at your institution, and if so, do your faculty and staff know about it?

## Step 3: Build Trust with Colleagues

When the department chair suspects that a mental health issue is causing job-related problems, having an ongoing trusting relationship with the faculty member provides the best basis for moving forward. Developing such relationships with all of your departmental colleagues should be well under way before you need to address job-related deficits, but psychologically impaired colleagues present special challenges.

Many behaviors associated with mental disorders make other people uncomfortable, and chairs may choose to avoid the problem by avoiding the troubled person, resulting in isolation for the psychologically impaired individual. The person's responses to colleagues may also contribute to his or her isolation. Suspicion and distrust are symptomatic of some disorders, such as schizophrenia. Individuals with other disorders may have a restricted ability to read emotional cues and interpret them correctly. For example, most colleagues will read your glancing at your watch as a sign that the conversation is winding down, whereas a psychologically impaired colleague may never even notice the signal. Individuals with brain disorders, developmental impairments, or early dementia may be unaware that they have become impaired, and others may be convinced that they are successfully concealing problems such as depression, anxiety, substance abuse, or mental deterioration. Finally, in settings with low tolerance for unusual behavior, faculty members are highly unlikely to self-disclose mental health issues due to embarrassment or fears of losing status or resources.

As the department chair, you need to be proactive about approaching individuals whom you suspect may be suffering from psychological impairments and get to know them. Building a reservoir of positive experiences makes difficult follow-up conversations easier. Noting individuals' positive accomplishments or just finding out about their outside interests may allow them to feel more comfortable with you and help you understand their strengths, not just their failings. Once you have this understanding, you can usually find ways to help your colleagues use their strengths and manage their issues for the betterment of students, colleagues, and the department. Defining departmental issues in terms of individual failings not only hurts the problem individual but also corrodes departmental trust as others wonder whether you will support them if they have problems in the future. View your colleagues as persons with genuine strengths that could lead them toward productive life patterns, whether in the department or not.

Clear, honest, and consistent communication is the essential basis for the development of trusting relationships with anyone, but it is particularly important in situations where mental health issues are involved. To communicate more effectively with psychologically impaired colleagues, you need to maintain an even emotional tone and send very concrete and specific messages. Marian was too distracted to see nonverbal signals and needed specific direction; for example, writing down one or two brief points for her in unambiguous language could have helped. But she was also a very creative individual who cared passionately about her discipline, the school, and the students. Helping her perceive needed changes as ways to express her passion and meet her students' needs might have helped her adapt more effectively.

The chair's messages also need to clearly reflect dual interests—in the faculty member's well-being and in the successful performance of the job. The more specifically you can identify these two issues, the more successful you are likely to be with a broad range of faculty. But however clear you are, realize that your message may become distorted as a result of psychological impairment. For example, an anxious or depressed faculty member is likely to interpret comments about job performance as personal criticism or as confirmation of a negative self-assessment. Faculty who are aware that their performance is deteriorating, whether due to encroaching psychotic thoughts or increasing brain dysfunction, are likely to be terrified and perceive negative comments about their job performance as confirmation of their worst fears. Showing them that you are interested in their personal well-being as well as their functioning in the job can be reassuring at a time of great stress and may unstick them enough to allow them to find a solution with you, rather than simply attempting to follow a directive from you that they cannot fully comprehend.

In some ways, faculty who have not faced their impairments are the most difficult to approach. You may be the first to verbalize the issues to a poorly performing colleague. That person may be fighting against recognition of loss of abilities and could react initially with anger and denial. Having a history of showing personal interest and caring can be helpful. It can also be important to stick to behaviors observed, rather than global judgments of competence, and to give that person time to grieve in the form of shock (no response), denial ("these are my excuses"), anger ("you have not explained it well"), and eventually, we hope, acceptance ("I celebrate what I did, and now I need a new direction in life").

## Step 4: Evaluate Yourself and Your Perceptions

What do you believe about mental disorders and impairment? What have your experiences been with psychological disability? How do those experiences and attitudes color your current relationships with faculty colleagues who may be psychologically impaired?

Discomfort with acknowledging the presence of a mental illness is widespread and often leads us to stay silent and overlook behaviors that could open the door to a more productive and caring conversation. "I noticed that you seemed sad this morning" may be a difficult sentence to utter, but if you do not, you lose the opportunity to build respect, trust, and confidence in your leadership. Even if you do notice and accept the presence of a colleague's psychological disability, it may be difficult to understand why the individual cannot just "snap out of it" or "let it go." After all, doesn't everyone get depressed sometimes? Failing to appreciate the impaired person's real inability to conform his or her thinking and behavior to social norms often leads us to become impatient and turn away from the relationship just when the individual needs support the most. As the department chair, consider that your problematic faculty colleague may want to behave differently but cannot due to a lack of the skills, biological makeup, or supportive environment needed to change. The person may not even be aware of the impact on you and on the department. It is helpful to step back from annoying or difficult behavior to see the person behind it while still understanding that particular work tasks need to be done.

Part of your self-assessment is honestly evaluating your resources for working with this person and being clear with yourself about the limits of your role as a colleague and an employer. Ultimately, the individual is responsible for the choices he or she makes, and you are not in a position to act as therapist (even if you wanted to!). You are not in a position to "save" an impaired colleague, but you may be able to provide appropriate support if you have the time, will, and talent. You may also be in the best position to make a meaningful referral to other resources who may be better placed for this work.

You are very likely to have had one or more important relationships in your life affected by some kind of mental impairment. Although knowing and interacting with psychologically impaired family members, friends, and colleagues can help you feel more comfortable in these situations, personal experience is a double-edged sword. Your perceptions of mental illness and individuals who suffer from it can be negatively skewed by a bad experience (causing you to conclude, say, that all addicts are liars or that all brain-injured individuals are hopeless). Another fallacy is to believe that your experience generalizes to the current situation (for example, if medications helped your sister-in-law, they should help your colleague too). If you are dealing with a colleague who shows the same maladaptive behaviors as someone with whom you have had an intense connection, it is particularly important to look closely at the unique qualities of this person and this situation, or you risk imposing your own attitudes and agenda. It is very important to talk to your supervisor or consult with a mental health professional if you find yourself in this position so that you can keep your own boundaries and thinking clear. Stepping back to look at the individual issues and behaviors involved in this specific instance can help minimize the negative impact of your prior experiences and assumptions. Marian's department chair does not appear to have considered his own possible issues and responses prior to taking action.

## Step 5: Listen

Observing behavior and listening to faculty concerns allows you to collect concrete, behavioral data with which to build an accurate assessment of the situation. Paying careful attention to the privacy of the individual in question, collect data from all persons involved in specific incidents. By examining the nature, timing, and context of problem behavior, you can gather clues that help you understand who or what may be triggering problem situations. As you collect these data, it's useful to look for an underlying logic or pattern to the individual's maladaptive behavior. Combining your observations with your knowledge of the individual's history can help you assemble a fuller picture of the problem that will let you come up with better strategies. For example, a senior faculty member who had received teaching awards over his career had recently begun acting erratically. He had emotional outbursts and made sexually suggestive comments to at least one female student. Students complained that his lectures made no sense. This abrupt change in behavior strongly suggested that some medical or psychological process was impairing his ability to function. The standard approach to such a problem would be to initiate disciplinary action, which would be ineffective if it was in fact a biological or mental health issue. In this particular case, after the chair documented the altered pattern of behavior and suggested a referral for medical and psychological evaluation, specialists determined that the individual had brain damage from a sports accident. The faculty member was placed on disability and was spared the disgrace that termination would have caused.

In Marian's case, Lawrence could have explored her history at the university and compared her prior work with her current problems. Given the apparently complex medical issues she was dealing with, it was possible that medications or treatment were making it hard for her to be organized. Patients are often unprepared for the psychological side effects of medicines, and given the heavy intellectual demands of faculty work, a side effect that does not affect a person with a less demanding job can undermine faculty performance. A proper evaluation of Marian's health situation might have uncovered a simple solution—change her medications—or supported the idea that it was not her health but long-standing behavioral issues that were responsible for her conduct.

### Documentation

As you gather information and assess your particular situation, do not overlook the importance of documenting your actions and your findings. In any delicate personnel matter, good documentation can make the difference between a satisfactory resolution and a court appearance.

Documentation should be done contemporaneously whenever possible. Doing so helps establish the sequence of events and activities, and writing things down while they are fresh in your mind also leads to greater accuracy than waiting until days or weeks later. Your notes should describe only what you see, hear, and do or what others do. Avoid subjective descriptive labels such as *sad, furious,* or *threatening;* instead, record actual words spoken, using quotation marks, and make it clear who is saying what and to whom. Keep your own opinions out of official records, and make sure that these records include only relevant information.

As you enter the action phase, suggestions, recommendations, or directions given to your subordinates should be carefully documented, as they may become the basis for litigation in difficult cases. Lawrence's notes about a meeting with Marian, several months into problem resolution, might have read something like this:

After 3 complaints from students about MK's class (see e-mail file), we met at a time that she said was convenient. I presented the e-mails to MK and asked her to comment. MK said that those 3 students "were always complaining." I asked her to suggest how she might address the specific complaints, and MK frowned and said, "I am not pandering to the lowest common denominator." I suggested that she think back to when she was a student and asked how she would have wanted her complaints handled. She paused, sighed loudly, and then said, "I see your point. I'll take care of it." I asked her to provide me with a written plan within 3 days after consultation with her mentor, and she agreed to do so. I sent a follow-up e-mail thanking her for meeting with me and repeating the expectations from the meeting, asking her to review and respond if this was not her understanding.

## Step 6: Take Effective Action

If you have decided that there is a problem that needs to be dealt with and that the problem may be caused or exacerbated by a psychological impairment, it is time to act. By the way, in Marian's case, Lawrence held one more disciplinary meeting with her following which there was no improvement. Marian was terminated midsemester. Perhaps we are left asking the question, Was this action suitably considerate as well as "right" for the department?

### *Is There a Possibility of Danger?*

This is a frightening possibility for most of us and is thankfully not common. But occasionally faculty colleagues do become dangerous to themselves or to others, and when they are emotionally charged, they are likely to engage your "inner lizard." Although predicting dangerousness is extremely difficult, what might make you feel that there is a potentially dangerous situation developing, and what might you be able to do?

Psychologically based problems may remain at a chronic low level over time and then suddenly flare, or they may present quickly and deteriorate rapidly. If you sense a shift in mood that makes you uneasy, do not brush off or avoid the issue. Similarly, if an individual who is already emotionally fragile has had a recent personal or professional loss, such as rejection of an important grant or publication, loss of status or position, or a negative change in family relationships, this may precipitate a mental health crisis.

If you have concerns about potential danger, it is important to cycle back to Step 2. What is the protocol at your university for dealing with potentially dangerous situations? If your university does not have a protocol, encourage appropriate campus officials, including the university's legal counsel, to create one before it is needed. Employee assistance counselors, campus mental health professionals, the Human Resource Department, deans and academic administrators, and the campus or community police may also need to be involved in this discussion. Although formulating this type of policy is clearly beyond the responsibilities of the department chair, you can point out the need for such a policy on your campus. Marian was not a danger to others and probably not to herself but may have had the potential for depression and suicide. If she had committed suicide, what might Lawrence have wished he had done as her chair?

When dealing with potentially dangerous colleagues, calm, nonjudgmental honesty is most effective. Share your concerns clearly and concretely, and then ask the individual to respond. You might say, "I'm really worried about you. . . . You seem so down when we talk, and your comments about giving away your books and not needing any office space for next semester concern me. I'm worried that you are thinking about hurting yourself. Are you?" With potentially suicidal individuals, you can get a rough idea of the seriousness of the threat by finding out what kind of planning the individual has done. Someone who vaguely refers to "not being around" is of less concern than someone who is armed and has decided on a location or a specific series of events. Both of these individuals are at risk; however, in the second situation, which is more acute, immediate steps (such as hospitalization or intervening with a member of the family) should be taken. Vague statements such as "I'd like to get that guy" are less troubling than actual stalking or threatening an intended victim. When your level of concern is low, you can try to refer the person for treatment by empathically repeating troubling things the person says and reinforcing the idea that seeking expert opinions and advice is a wise course of action.

If your attempts to help fail or if you believe that dangerous behavior is possible, it is time to get others involved. You could arrange a meeting with the faculty member and a respected third party such as the dean, someone from human resources, or a counselor. Having others with you is helpful for a variety of reasons. If the faculty member changes earlier statements in the presence of others, you can repeat what was said and describe the behaviors that led to your concerns. The faculty member's first response may be anger, but at this point, safety is your paramount concern. Although people usually appreciate a helping hand when they are in distress, that appreciation may be delayed or absent when working with psychologically impaired colleagues. On the other hand, try not to make the situation worse. Be cognizant that the body language and arrangement of those present can feel threatening if they appear too aggressively lined up against the individual. If you want police nearby, don't have them sitting in a visible location, as that may be the trigger to cause the situation to deteriorate. In an ideal situation, the faculty member will feel that at least one person in the room is on his or her side.

Very rarely, an immediate and strongly credible threat (such as the presence of a weapon) may occur. Now your top priority is protecting yourself and others. Should you ever find yourself in this position (and the vast majority of us never will), use nonthreatening body language and vocal tones, and avoid moving into the individual's space. A calm, unhurried body posture and tone of voice signals to the other person that he or she can also be calm.

### When the Situation Is Not Dangerous

If dangerous behavior is not a concern and you have determined that you need to address an issue with a psychologically impaired colleague, initiate a conversation as soon as possible so that the faculty member will feel respected and included in the process. Avoid comments that are based on personal judgments (for example, "You were rude to Jim in the department meeting"). Describing behaviors that need to change (advice to soften volume, tone, or body language) and focusing on how to change either the behaviors or the situation allow you to address problems without unnecessarily labeling the individual. Focus on specific examples: for example, "Marian, students tell me that you have lost papers at least three times and that you have not shown up to class four times this month." Then stop and give her a chance to respond. Listening carefully and restating what you heard shows that you are paying attention to the speaker's concerns. "So you're missing your morning class because you keep forgetting to set your alarm clock and oversleeping, is that correct?" Once you have jointly identified and agreed on the issues of concern, your discussion can move to possible interventions. Encourage the individual to generate a solution that is focused on the specific goal behavior: "What can you do from here on to be present in every class on time?" Such questions leave the faculty member in charge and working with you rather than against you. They help you understand more clearly the person with whom you are dealing. Your input is also necessary to determine an acceptable outcome for this situation. What could the department and you as chair live with? Is this approach realistic? Is the outcome acceptable to the challenged faculty member as well?

With individuals who are disorganized and flighty in their speech, identifying specific behaviors and solutions can be challenging and require several attempts. It can be done, however, one small concrete step at a time. If the faculty member is able to generate a viable plan, you have some cause for optimism. Vague or ineffective plans suggest that the issues are going to be harder to resolve. If those plans fail, then it will be appropriate to help the individual realize that his or her problem is too big to be solved easily without outside help.

If the problem is mainly in the classroom, referring the individual to your faculty development office (if you have one) can be beneficial. This referral should be framed as a choice that the faculty member can make to improve his or her teaching. Often an observation or videotape of a class session by someone from outside the department can provide the safe space the faculty member needs to consider making changes. Of course, the final determination of whether acceptable outcomes have been achieved remains with you.

Many individuals with a wide variety of psychological issues share a difficulty in managing change, so it is important to be very clear about the process you plan to use to address problems and to stick to that process very closely. This is easiest if you have already thought through the process and addressed your own worries and concerns prior to your first contact with the faculty member, as in Step 4. Remember that the individual may need to go through the several stages of grief before recognizing and accepting the current problem and that this generally does not happen in one

> *Many individuals with a wide variety of psychological issues share a difficulty in managing change.*

interview. What will you do if the faculty member denies the problem or blames a colleague? What if the person breaks down in your meeting? What if he or she becomes angry at you? What if your colleague agrees with you and comes up with a viable plan? Will you be disappointed because your preferred outcome is really for the person to leave the department? Staying focused on the individual's strengths and maintaining an even emotional tone is much easier if you have anticipated and planned for all likely possibilities and for your own reactions to them.

Marian had worked at the university for many years prior to becoming a faculty member, and that may have complicated her relationships within the department. Lawrence may not have understood that the transition between two very different roles would not be smooth. Neither Lawrence nor Marian may have anticipated how radically her world would change. Previously positive relationships may have made it harder to intervene earlier as both Marian and Lawrence assumed they had the sort of relationship necessary for success when in actuality it was based on different work roles. Thinking through the situation might have allowed Lawrence to approach her comfortably, make positive statements about her past work, and encourage her to seek more help.

Several potential outcomes may arise in situations with underlying mental health components:

- **The problem may be short-term and easily resolved** by frank discussion with the chair with or without support from faculty developers, employee assistance providers, counselors, or others. Relatively acute or treatable impairments, such as grief relating to the death of a spouse are more likely to result in quick recovery. Sensitive handling of such situations builds trust and goodwill throughout the department.

- **The problem may be chronic and resistant to change.** Attempts to change are promised but do not occur or are unsuccessful. The ensuing conversation about why the faculty member is unable to change his or her behavior to meet departmental expectations may lead to acknowledgment that more help is needed or that the job is just too much to handle at this time. The supportive chair can suggest strategies such as a temporary leave or course reduction, changing the work environment where possible, providing additional support during high-stress periods, or finding another position. Consulting with the dean and the campus ADA coordinator is an important part of this process, as the department chair alone usually cannot make such accommodations. Marian's situation fell into this category. Lawrence undoubtedly felt that he had tried to accommodate Marian's problems but that she was unable to change. When all reasonable avenues have been explored and there is no change, disciplinary actions may be required, as in Marian's case. However, before the loss of a formerly valuable colleague, this should only come after a very thorough consideration of all the possibilities. If Marian's problems were triggered by her medications, a change in them might have helped. She might have been eligible for short- or long-term disability, depending on campus policies. Marian's problems were not fully explored, so we cannot know if the disciplinary action was appropriate.

- **The problem may become acute and critical.** You may begin to see deterioration or wide fluctuations in behavior or emotional state, or you may see signs of danger that did not exist before. Recognizing the downhill trend, stepping aside from the situation, and making appropriate referrals may end up being the most effective steps we can take for some individuals. Again, consulting with human resources, employee assistance, and your supervisor is critical in assessing your options and respecting the rights of all parties.

## ∿ A Final Word ∿

Working with psychologically impaired faculty may feel like an overwhelming addition to your busy life as a department chair, but you are already doing so, whether you are aware of it or not. If you can find constructive ways to manage and support these colleagues, you will have a skill set that works with anyone. According to management expert Peter Drucker, "The task of leadership is to create an alignment of strengths in ways that make the system's weaknesses *irrelevant.*"[9] By becoming aware of the signs and symptoms of distress, you can intervene in respectful, meaningful, and effective ways that will result in a departmental system where faculty get the respect and support they need, students get the high-quality education they deserve, and colleagues enjoy a productive and constructive departmental work environment.

### Summary for Dealing with the Psychologically Impaired

- Become familiar with the basic signs of psychological impairment, and know whom to contact when you sense you need help.

- Clarify departmental values (and essential job functions) so that you can see and clarify the gap between behavior and expectations.

- Check out the Americans with Disabilities Act, and look into how your university implements its provisions.

- Be proactive in warmly approaching individuals whom you suspect may be suffering from psychological

*(Continued)*

impairments, and get to know them (but realize that your interaction may be misunderstood as a result of their psychological inadequacies).

- Be mindful of your own biases; don't generalize or assume that you understand a psychologically challenged colleague based on your own experience.

- Document your observations and interactions promptly; keep good records.

- Rely on the professionals on your campus to assist you; if there is any indication of danger to you, your colleague, or others, seek immediate help.

# Notes

1. J. Lacey. (2005). Prevalence and severity of mental illness in the United States. *Archives of General Psychiatry, 62*, 590–592. Retrieved from http://www.eurekalert.org/pub_releases/2005-06/jaaj-pas060205.php

2. D. Schwebel. (2009). Impaired faculty: Helping academics who are suffering from serious mental illness. *Academic Leadership, 7*(2). Retrieved from http://www.docstoc.com/docs/83410407/Impaired-Faculty-Helping-Academics-Who-Are-Suffering-from-Serious

3. A. H. Winefield & R. Jarrett. (2001). Occupational stress in university staff. *International Journal of Stress Management, 8*(4), 285–298.

4. G. Kinman. (2001). Pressure points: A review of research on stressors and strains in UK academics. *Educational Psychology, 21*(4), 473–492. doi:10.1080/01443410120090849

5. J. Ruark. (2010, February 16). In academe, mental health issues are hard to recognize and hard to treat. *Chronicle of Higher Education*. Retrieved from http://chronicle.com/article/In-Academe-Mental-Health-I/64246/

6. J. C. Dunn, W. J. Whelton, & D. Sharpe. (2006). Maladaptive perfectionism, hassles, coping, and psychological distress in university professors. *Journal of Counseling Psychology, 53*(4), 511–523.

7. Code of Federal Regulations. (2011). *Part 1630: Regulations to implement the Equal Employment Opportunity provisions of the Americans with Disabilities Act.* Retrieved from http://www.gpo.gov/fdsys/pkg/CFR-2011-title29-vol4/xml/CFR-2011-title29-vol4-part1630.xml

8. B. A. Lee & P. R. Ruger. (2003). *Accommodating faculty and staff with psychiatric disabilities.* Washington, DC: National Association of College and University Attorneys.

9. P. Drucker, quoted in D. L. Cooperrider & L. N. Godwin. (2010, August 26). *Positive organization development: Innovation-inspired change in an economy and ecology of strengths.* Retrieved from http://appreciativeinquiry.case.edu/intro/IPOD_draft_8-26-10.pdf

# Conclusion

I began this book by pointing out that its claim was not six *easy* steps for dealing with problem faculty. Working with people whose style and preferences differ markedly from ours, particularly if they deviate from standard or acceptable performance, is always challenging. But rising to this challenge is a large part of what good chairing is all about. Many are the chairs who attest to the satisfaction of helping establish a more functional department, one that knows and honors high standards, one that is more fun to come to each morning, one that laughs and celebrates together, and one that feels gratitude for the chair who upon stepping down leaves behind a terrific climate for the next chair to inherit.

Do not be discouraged if you feel that you or your department is off course. I'm told that when an airplane traverses any flight, it is off course 99 percent of the time. But by making continual corrections, by following the rules, by drawing on the advice of copilots and experts, and by slowing down a little when there is turbulence, each pilot is able to successfully land the plane on the intended runway. In the same way, by thoughtful reflection, practice, involvement of others, and course corrections based on these six steps, you'll take your department to a positive place.

I offer four specific encouragements:

- **If you're a new chair** and you struggle with problem behavior of some of your faculty, make alleviating this issue a priority for your tenure. You may not be able to stop it, but you could do much during your term to greatly diminish it.
- **If you're midstream in your chairing term** and you're now aware of one or more problem faculty situations, you have an ideal opportunity to say "OK, I've had some experience. I know the territory. I see what's well received and what isn't. I'll call on my trusted colleagues to help me; we will tackle this now."
- **If you're a veteran chair** and your department has this problem, don't leave it on the shelf. Get things started, or finish what has already begun. The next chair won't have your years of experience and wisdom.
- **If you don't have a problem faculty challenge** in your department, celebrate that. Declare specifically what it is that you value, and clarify how your department will preserve and sustain such a state.

Good luck!

# Sample Vision and Mission
# Statement

# Sacred Heart University Graduate Program in Occupational Therapy

## PROGRAM'S VISION

The Occupational Therapy Program faculty adopted a vision that embodies the values and goals of the program, its curriculum, the faculty and staff, and students.

### *P.R.I.D.E.*

*We are:*

PRINCIPLED

- Our day-to-day operations and long-term planning are in accordance with our mission, vision, professional ethics, and core values.
- Our values reflect the University's mission.
- Occupational justice is a departmental priority; it includes service to the local community, especially the uninsured, poor, children, and women.

RESPONSIVE

- The program strives to be responsive to the needs of the community, the poor, and the elderly.
- The program strives to be responsive to changing professional and societal trends and technology.
- The program strives to be readily available and personally attend to the needs of our students, staff, and faculty and operate in a student-centered manner.
- The program strives to provide continuing education to the occupational therapy community, adjunct faculty, PBL facilitators, and fieldwork educators.

## INNOVATIVE

- The program's cutting-edge curriculum is reflective of its vision, mission, professional, and health care needs.
- The program utilizes cutting-edge pedagogies and includes a semester dedicated to building foundational skills and knowledge, student portfolio, therapeutic use of self-curriculum, and problem-based learning.
- The faculty is open to critical questioning of existing models, frames of reference, and domains of knowledge.
- The program is among the first in the University to implement cutting-edge technologies for learning and daily operation.
- The faculty is dedicated to staying current in educational practice, clinical advancements, research, and technology.

## DYNAMIC

- The program faculty are collaborative and team-oriented and strive for diversity and dynamism in pedagogy, clinical expertise, and educational approach.
- Faculty seek and encourage multiple, diverse perspectives to solve problems.
- Faculty are flexible, adaptable to changing needs and advances, and responsive to changes in practice, health care needs and environments, and the profession.
- Faculty are dedicated to seeking diversity in faculty, staff, and student populations.
- Faculty are knowledgeable and committed to lifelong learning.

*(Continued)*

## Sacred Heart University Graduate Program in Occupational Therapy (*Continued*)

EXCELLENT
- The faculty are well respected in the professional community. They provide service to the community, engage in continual curricular improvements and innovative design, and are committed to quality teaching, scholarship, and leadership in the profession.
- Our NBCOT pass rate is above the national average.
- Our faculty are committed to developing professional leaders who serve.
- Faculty members strive for curricular excellence, quality teaching, and engagement in scholarship.

### PROGRAM'S MISSION

The mission of the Graduate Program in Occupational Therapy at Sacred Heart University is to prepare men and women to enter the profession of occupational therapy with the knowledge, skills, and personal values that will enable them to serve in a manner that exemplifies professional excellence and true humanity.

As a learning community rooted in the Catholic intellectual tradition, we are committed to giving personal attention to each student in order to foster in them:

- Facility to move among different cultures with an open mind and respect for the diversity of the human family
- Ability to reflect on and articulate their own beliefs and assumptions

- Desire to contribute to the common good as persons and as professionals
- Active engagement in promoting a just society through professional practice, leadership, and scholarship

We believe that:

- Every human being has dignity and worth
- Each person has an inherent right to engage fully in his or her daily occupations in order to realize his or her highest potential
- A compassionate heart is essential in all interactions with clients and communities of need
- Ethical practice and moral citizenship are fundamental responsibilities

We promote a learning environment that:

- Values diverse educational backgrounds as well as the values of a liberal arts education
- Forms collaborative partnerships between faculty, students, and clinical practitioners
- Promotes a culture of rigorous scholarly inquiry
- Expects a commitment to lifelong learning

Our approach to learning is to:

- Create an educational experience that forges the sharp edge of critical thinking
- Model the continuous pursuit of knowledge and truth

*(Continued)*

## Sacred Heart University Graduate Program in Occupational Therapy (*Continued*)

- Encourage the development of each student's particular talents and gifts
- Foster clinical reasoning and evidence-based practice through self-directed, problem-based learning

Courtesy of Judy Bortone, Department of Occupational Therapy and Health Sciences, Sacred Heart University, Fairfield, Connecticut

# APPENDIX B

# Sample No-Bullying Policy

Approved by: [name of institution, department, committee]

Date of Approval: _____

Contact Person: _____

The University of _____ is committed to maintaining a workplace that is free from bullying and related behaviors, a workplace where all people are treated with courtesy and respect. We define bullying as any action that offends, intimidates, humiliates, ridicules, demeans, undermines, or threatens another individual, especially if it undermines the person's physical or emotional health. Such conduct is unacceptable and will not be tolerated.

Examples of bullying may include but are not limited to the following:

- Threats or actual violence
- Aggressive, abusive, or offensive language including vulgarity
- Unnecessary physical contact
- Recurring nonconstructive or excessive criticism
- Hounding or disproportionate scrutiny
- Ridicule, scorn, teasing, mocking
- Being asked to do trivial, unpleasant work including that below your level of competence
- Being isolated, shunned, ignored, rejected, or excluded from normal activities
- Having information or entitlements afforded others withheld from you
- Having fabrications made about or against you

Bullying is typically committed by a person who is relatively more powerful against a person who is less powerful either in status or personality, and it leaves the targeted person feeling less secure, less respected, less energized, and less welcome at work. Thus the best person to determine when bullying is occurring is the victim, not the perpetrator or even a bystander. It is therefore important that any employee who feels that he or she is being bullied be granted a receptive audience with the contact person identified above and that this person not dismiss or negate the validity of the victim's assertion. In addition, it is essential that any department employee who comes forward with a concern about bullying, either as a witness or as a victim, not be retaliated against by the alleged bully or by any others.

Bona fide bullying normally consists of a recurring pattern of conduct. Bullying may be perpetrated by or against either gender. An isolated incident is not considered bullying but may warrant discipline. Conducting performance evaluations or peer reviews or enacting disciplinary procedures does not in and of itself constitute bullying. Constructive feedback and comments are expected in the carrying out of university business but must be done in a way that does not demean or humiliate.

Anyone who bullies will be subject to discipline, which could consist of a verbal admonition, a formal written warning, probation, a decrease in pay, or loss of employment.

# APPENDIX C

# Faculty Behaviors That May Suggest a Mental Health Problem

The examples given here are meant to help you look more closely at underlying reasons for some difficult behaviors. This table is *not* a diagnostic tool, and you should never use diagnostic terms with colleagues. The examples are based on the authors' experiences only. Remember that a mental health problem is an extreme version of behaviors all of us engage in. Individuals without mental health problems may display these behaviors, and individuals with the same disorder may display a different set of behaviors. Highly intelligent persons are able to compensate and cover up better than most, navigating the school system and only encountering problems in the less structured work environment.

| Signs and Symptoms as a Clinician Sees Them | Behaviors You May See in the Department |
| --- | --- |
| **Anxiety Disorders (including phobias, panic disorder, obsessive-compulsive disorder, and posttraumatic stress disorder)** | |
| Excessive worrying, repetitive behaviors, frequent illnesses, obvious tension, being easily startled, talking too much or too rapidly, reluctance to travel or change routines, avoidance of certain situations. | Talks too rapidly or too long in meetings or in class |
| | Provides excessive details in materials; seeks perfection rather than excellence |
| Rigidity and perfectionism, moralistic attitudes, feeling overwhelmed, inability to "let go" of tasks, expectations, etc. | Is overly rigid about class or departmental rules |
| | Expresses feelings of overwhelming stress under typical work conditions |
| | Avoids taking part in new initiatives |
| | Is reluctant to participate in campus outreach, going to a different campus, or teaching after dark |
| | Overreacts to student acts of plagiarism and cheating |

*(Continued)*

May feel easily threatened by students or colleagues (including you) and be unable to respond calmly

May function adequately as long as the routine remains the same but has difficulty coping in a new situation (such as a change of teaching assignment)

Focuses tightly on details

## Mood Disorders (including major depression, dysthymia, bipolar disorder, cyclothymia, and seasonal affective disorder)

*If depressed:*
Flat or sad affect, low energy, fatigue, problems concentrating, excessive guilt, thoughts of death or references to dying or not being around

Loss of interest in things that were formerly pleasurable or engaging

Changes in weight (gain or loss) and eating habits, change in sleeping habits, restlessness or psychomotor slowing

No hostile or bizarre behavior

*If bipolar:*

Depressive periods alternating with periods of manic symptoms such as agitation or high energy, excessively high self-esteem, talkativeness, distractibility, charm, outgoing nature, unrestrained behavior, racing thoughts, or intense irritation

Mood swings that cycle rapidly or more slowly and may be moderate or so extreme as to appear psychotic

*If depressed:*
Is highly disorganized, unable to concentrate on course activities

Gives up; dismisses classes early or doesn't show up

Expresses hopelessness

Does not make progress on scholarship or other commitments; misses multiple meetings and appointments without much of an excuse ("Just can't seem to get going")

*If bipolar:*

Behaves inconsistently, sometimes showing the behaviors cited for depression and at other times the following:

Is overly talkative in classes or meetings, and content may be illogical or unfocused

Is distracted by every new idea

May make exuberant promises to students, make wild claims, or start grandiose projects that never get done

Thinks creatively and thoughtfully and can focus on long-term issues when health is good

*(Continued)*

| Signs and Symptoms as a Clinician Sees Them | Behaviors You May See in the Department |
|---|---|
| **Impulse Control Disorders** | |
| Loss of control<br><br>Multiple angry or hostile outbursts out of proportion to any provocation that may result in damage to property or assault | Loses control—for example, throws student papers on the floor or screams at a colleague or student |
| **Substance Abuse** | |
| Evidence of use (smell or stains) during the workday<br><br>Appearing hung over or under the influence at work<br><br>Disappearing without explanation<br><br>A pattern of unreliable or erratic behavior and flimsy excuses<br><br>Unkempt appearance<br><br>*Note:* Some prescription medications for other conditions, such as migraines, can produce similar effects to these or to those of brain trauma (see below). | Repeatedly misses classes and meetings, always with excuses, eventually not very believable ones<br><br>May come to class hung over or under the influence<br><br>Appears disheveled or wears odd attire such as sunglasses when indoors or long sleeves during hot weather<br><br>May avoid morning classes and meetings<br><br>Attends to course and departmental obligations erratically<br><br>Doesn't remember conversations or duties |
| **Schizophrenia Family** | |
| Odd behaviors such as talking to self, making comments that don't make sense, acting as though others know things that they do not, believing that someone is out to get them, seeming to hear voices or see things that are not there, becoming agitated, or acting bizarre or hostile | Is distracted in lecture—disorganized and wandering in a disconnected manner<br><br>Is difficult to follow in conversation, not because the content is challenging but because there are few or no connecting explanations<br><br>May hop from topic to topic on the basis of how the words sound (e.g., jumping from a discussion of the ego to eagles) |

*(Continued)*

Lack of expected behaviors, such as failing to maintain personal hygiene, showing flat or inappropriate affect, reduced motivation, withdrawing from people, or disinterest in important relationships

Has difficulty reading or responding to the emotional states of students and colleagues

May withdraw from classes, research, and other activities

May comment on voices or other experiences that do not seem to have a basis in reality

May display increasingly unusual behavior during times of stress (e.g., midterms, finals, due dates)

May function appropriately as long as the routine remains constant but is extremely sensitive to change

## Dementias (including Alzheimer's)

Increasing forgetfulness, initially covered with anger or denial; swearing that something was done or turned in but was not

Noticeable difficulty recalling recent memories

*Note:* Some organic brain disorders (e.g., stroke) may have similar symptoms.

Functions less and less well over time

May be easily angered when asked for missing work

Does not recall what was covered in class; may repeat self

May do half of a task and forget the rest of it

May function appropriately as long as the routine remains constant but is extremely sensitive to change

## Brain Trauma (from stroke or accident)

(This is not a mental health disorder, but the behaviors may resemble one.)

Poor impulse control

Poor attention span and odd inconsistencies in performance (e.g., manages to grade one stack of papers but can't handle the next one)

Is unable to maintain prior levels of functioning, resulting in incomplete syllabi or directions for students and papers that pile up ungraded

May complain about being easily distracted

May seek to maintain a simpler, more structured environment, appearing uncooperative

*(Continued)*

| Signs and Symptoms as a Clinician Sees Them | Behaviors You May See in the Department |
|---|---|
| Blackouts or abrupt changes in handwriting or other skills | May begin behaving impulsively—for example, having outbursts in class or making inappropriate sexual advances |
| *Note:* Because the typical academic's work requires processing complex cognitive tasks, what would be a mild impairment in another person may result in significant work impairment for the academic, something the medical system may fail to recognize. Also, depression can follow, especially if no one recognizes the problem. | Shows a high need for structure and routine and cannot function adequately in unfamiliar environments or situations |

### Learning Disabilities

| | |
|---|---|
| Functioning in a specific academic area grossly below the individual's level of functioning in other academic areas | Resists mathematical grading schemes and makes errors of calculation (indicative of a learning disability in math) |
| | Sidesteps committee assignments with a lot of reading or resists assigning papers to students (indicative of a learning disability in reading) |
| | *Note:* Problems with reading or writing may result in inadequate scholarly output. |

### Attention Deficit Disorder (with or without hyperactivity) (ADD and ADHD)

| | |
|---|---|
| Inability to focus when required, particularly on less interesting tasks | Has difficulty getting and staying organized or finishing work |
| Focusing too tightly on some tasks or subjects | Has difficulty monitoring exams or other tasks requiring close attention |
| Hyperactive behavior (especially in males) or else appearing quietly distracted | Struggles to complete reports, scholarship, and grading in a timely manner |
| | May lack social skills |

*(Continued)*

Focuses obsessively on details of one particular area (for example, in a specialty) but is otherwise unfocused and distracted in a manner similar to the inconsistency following brain trauma

## Asperger's Syndrome

Difficulty interpreting the behaviors of others, especially emotional situations, although this can improve with time

Desiring friends but not knowing how to get them

Avoiding eye contact or staring

Extreme attachment to routines and rules

Expressing thoughts without appropriate self-restraint

Narrow and egocentric focus on some aspect of intellectual achievement

Poor planning skills, difficulty following instructions, and excessive sensitivity to sensory stimuli

Depression or anxiety when not in a peer group

Has difficulty reading the emotional tone of the classroom

Responds best to explanations such as "If you want $x$, the way to get it is $y$" and "It's the rule"

Engages in long monologues (can be returned to the topic with "Thank you, but anyway ...")

Responds negatively to any change in routine

May look awkward physically, and deliver lectures that are deep in content but provide no opportunity for reflection or response

May have difficulty following university policies and may irritate departmental colleagues

# Acknowledgments

At this I will be inadequate; thanking or even remembering all of the people whose words and examples have influenced the writing of this book will not be possible. When it comes to chairing, I am indebted to Herb Johnson, Jim Ozbun, and Orvin Burnside, who, as my department heads, taught me ever so much more by their examples than they could possibly appreciate. I'm indebted to my many colleagues who endured and supported me while I was their department head at the University of Minnesota; their patience, criticisms, and numerous suggestions as they interacted with me helped me greatly and fashioned my attitudes and paradigms.

I'm especially indebted to the chairs and associates who served with me while I was a dean at Brigham Young University. Steve Taylor stands out; as a veteran assistant dean, he was my lone mentor as I struggled to launch my deanship following the retirement of the previous dean and his two associate deans on the very day of my arrival. Mark Rowe and Richard Tolman also wisely and kindly tutored me early on. The several directors, chairs, associate deans, and others who served with me each taught me (or experienced with me) something that made its way into this book: Marla Allred, John Bell,

Francesca Forsyth, Alan Harker, Paul Johnston, Von Jolley, David Kooyman (who took a hit for me that he shouldn't have had to, which I will always appreciate and never forget), John Lee, Sheldon Nelson, Lynn Ogden, Jim Porter, Sue Pratley, Ward Rees, Lonnie Riggs, Bruce Roundy, Larry Saint Clair, Duane Smith, Richard Thwaits, Kyle Tresner, Don Wright, and Shauna Anderson Young.

I was amazed and am very appreciative of the almost three thousand American department chairs who responded to my survey, most with written comments. It was their feedback that prompted me to write this book, which would not have happened but for the assistance of Sheryl Fullerton of Jossey-Bass, who rescued me from being bogged down in it all. I am delighted to be joined as authors by Carolyn Oxenford and Sally Kuhlenschmidt, who wrote Chapter Eleven; they were a delight to work with.

I thank Brigham Young University for supporting this project. Key people were Gary Reynolds and Brent Webb, who provided assistance for the initial survey. The encouragement of my current colleagues, Muriel Allen, Jane Birch, Jenith Larsen, and Dave Whetten, is appreciated. Special mention goes to Katie Barlow, the undergraduate student assistant who waded through and organized the survey results, my initial notes, and my several drafts, only to graduate and move on to her first "real" job on the very day that I write this.

My wife Gayle has been a helpful sweetheart throughout my career; she encouraged, accommodated, and waited up for me in her special way, for which I'm most appreciative.

R.K.C.

# The Author

**R. Kent Crookston** was raised on a wheat and dairy farm in Magrath, Alberta, Canada. He received his bachelor's degree in agronomy from Brigham Young University in 1968 and his Ph.D. in plant physiology from the University of Minnesota in 1972. He held postdoctoral positions with Agriculture Canada in Lethbridge, Alberta, and with Cornell University.

For twenty-four years he was a member of the agronomy faculty at the University of Minnesota, where he served as founding director of the Minnesota Institute of Sustainable Agriculture and as head of the Department of Agronomy and Plant Genetics. For two years he worked for the U.S. Agency for International Development in Morocco at the Hassan II Institute of Agriculture and Veterinary Sciences. Over twenty years he periodically consulted in the area of international development, primarily in Africa.

In 1998 Crookston joined Brigham Young University (BYU) as the dean of the College of Biology and Agriculture. Since 2007 he has directed the academic administrative support program at the BYU Faculty Center. In addition to researching academic administration, he researches and teaches effective decision making.

# Index

# More Resources for Department Chairs

**www.departmentchairs.org**

At a time in higher education when department chairs are faced with reduced budgets and increasingly demanding responsibilities, Jossey-Bass is proud to offer a wide range of distinctive resources tailored to your specific needs.

We've taken the guesswork out of assembling your one-stop-shop for professional enrichment through a diverse selection of books, newsletters, and online events.

Our goals:

- To provide the highest quality and most practical and relevant resources for department chairs at all academic institutions
- To design, develop, and deliver content in the most efficient and useful manner possible—in books, in periodicals, and in online seminars
- To foster a sense of community and connection among department chairs across all kinds of academic institutions
- To play a significant role in equipping department chairs with the information they need to provide excellent leadership

Visit **www.departmentchairs.org** to learn more about our book series, *The Department Chair* journal, electronic newsletter, online training, and other resources.

# Also available from Jossey-Bass

Time Management for Department Chairs

Christian K. Hansen

---

Paper, 160 pages, $30
ISBN 978-0-470-76901-0

---

The Department Chair Primer
*What Chairs Need to Know and Do to Make a Difference*
Second Edition

Don Chu

---

Paper, 128 pages, $30
ISBN 978-1-1180-7744-3

---

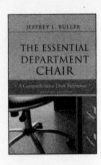

The Essential Department Chair
*A Comprehensive Desk Reference*
Second Edition

Jeffrey L. Buller

Cloth, 496 pages, $45
ISBN 978-1-1181-2374-4

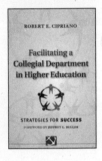

Facilitating a Collegial Department
in Higher Education
*Strategies for Success*

Robert E. Cipriano

Cloth, 224 pages, $40
ISBN 978-0-470-90301-8